TWELVE WAYS TO BUILD A VOCABULARY

*the text of this book is printed
on 100% recycled paper*

TWELVE WAYS TO BUILD
A VOCABULARY

By
ARCHIBALD HART, M.A., PH.D.

*With a Foreword by
Johnson O'Connor*

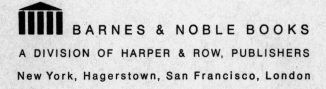

BARNES & NOBLE BOOKS

A DIVISION OF HARPER & ROW, PUBLISHERS

New York, Hagerstown, San Francisco, London

FOREWORD

CURIOSITY is a valuable stimulus to learning. Repetitious exercises may increase a student's vocabulary, but a genuine interest in words will make vocabulary building a pleasure and a treasure hunt, a pastime which will persist long after school requirements must be met.

The technique of vocabulary measurement now permits a reliable and accurate measure of an individual's vocabulary, but the stimulation of growth rather than the measurement of size is the real purpose of education. In perfecting the technique of vocabulary measurement the value of a large vocabulary in making the most of one's ability has been brought out repeatedly. A limited vocabulary limits both comprehension and expression, restricting and confining the possible use of one's powers. As a result, many attempts to perfect a technique of vocabulary building are being made throughout the country.

Dr. Hart's *Twelve Ways to Build a Vocabulary* is an interesting contribution to the present literature available on programs of vocabulary building. The pursuit of synonyms, antonyms, and Latin derivations has already been among the methods employed, but too often they have been the basis of tedious and per-functory drill. Dr. Hart's premise is that words are fascinating, and his presentation of information and questions makes them so and should arouse the curiosity cf even the least interested student.

All of Dr. Hart's suggested ways to build a vocabulary lead one inevitably to the dictionary. A capable teacher may thus use the book to encourage a habit which is probably inseparable from the acquisition of a rich and varied vocabulary. And for those who are already confirmed dictionary addicts, this volume will lure them more frequently to the dictionary and suggest new methods of browsing therein.

Twelve Ways to Build a Vocabulary combines the zest of a game with the discipline of a martinet. One is led into vocabulary improvement by opportunities to smile condescendingly at the errors of others, only to find oneself vulnerable and in search of a dictionary. Word-consciousness and curiosity once roused, vocabulary improvement is no longer a chore but an adventure. Curiosity once whetted will carry on the improvement of vocabulary long after the book has been finished.

JOHNSON O'CONNOR

CONTENTS

CONTENTS

INTRODUCTION

THIS book has been prepared for the use of those who appreciate the value of a large and accurate vocabulary. Others (if there are others) should consider that words are not only our principal means of communication with one another but are also the tools with which we do much of our thinking and, in a sense, are the very material out of which we make our thoughts. As a consequence the accuracy, flexibility, scope, and subtlety of one's thinking depend directly upon the same qualities of his vocabulary. There is evidence, furthermore, that words are stimulants to thought — that the presence of a word in the passive vocabulary can suggest to the mind a turn in the active thinking. And finally if these recommendations be not sufficient to convince the strictly practical, it should be remembered that a man's financial success is closely connected with the size of his vocabulary. Those interested in the economic advantages of a large and accurate vocabulary should read the famous article by Johnson O'Connor entitled "Vocabulary and Success" first printed in the *Atlantic Monthly* and often reprinted.

The natural way to acquire a good vocabulary is to absorb words steadily from much reading. Those who in their childhood have progressed, for instance, through *Alice* and George MacDonald and Kenneth Grahame to Stevenson, the most fastidious of word-lovers, and thence to the classics of English and American literature, will already have a good store of words and when they come to this book will find it all the easier to enlarge their vocabularies. It is obvious, however, that young people today give comparatively little time to reading, distracted as they are by amusements and pastimes in which the word is merely incidental or in which the verbal standard is low. The need for such a book as this is therefore greater than it was in an earlier generation.

The twelve ways of building vocabulary which are recommended and pursued in the chapters that follow are not the products of detached theorizing but have been used with success in classes of varying ages and in work with individual students. This book, if used with some industry, will accelerate one's immediate absorption of word-meanings and at the same time will prepare a soil in which vocabulary may strike deep root and grow continuously. Most of the book will prove useful to anyone — adult or child — no matter how large or small his present vocabulary.

The "Twelve Ways" of this book have been preferred to others because of their practicability and interest. Such a variety of methods is assurance that if one method should fail to catch the fancy of a student, eleven other possibilities remain of his finding an interesting approach. The study of words, however, should

INTRODUCTION

be more than interesting, for words have a charm and a romance to which few are insensitive. Indeed, students of all ages from elementary school to college — and older ones too — find the study of words a pleasure, for in the pursuit of synonyms, antonyms, definitions, and derivations, and in the recognition of Malapropisms, doublets, and idioms there is no small element of play. Browsing in a dictionary or in such a book as *Roget's Thesaurus* is fun, and one of the chapters of this book is appropriately entitled "Fun with the Dictionary and other Wordbooks."

The ten vocabulary tests and their keys, which appear at the back of the book, are the work of Thomas Lee Lipscomb, of the Gilman Country School, Baltimore, Maryland. They are difficult tests — purposely so — and are to be looked upon as instruments for vocabulary-building rather than as conventional classroom tests, and as games for groups.

ARCHIBALD HART

PUBLISHER'S NOTE

In order that you may get the greatest possible value out of this book, we make the following suggestions:

1. Be sure to read Johnson O'Connor's "Foreword" and the author's "Introduction" before starting the book.

2. You will probably find it helpful to read the chapter entitled "Fun with the Dictionary and Other Word-books," which begins on page 71, before you read Chapter I. In this chapter, the author gives detailed instructions on the use of a dictionary and lists other Word-books that are useful in the study of words and vocabulary-building.

3. The only reference book that is actually needed in connection with *Twelve Ways to Build a Vocabulary* is a good desk-size dictionary, but a Dictionary of Synonyms and Antonyms and Roget's *Thesaurus* will also prove useful.

4. In working out the exercises in Chapters VII, VIII and IX it will be helpful to have an etymological dictionary at hand.

5. If you will follow Dr. Hart's recommendations in his chapter on "Fun with the Dictionary," you will be much better equipped to experiment with the exercises that appear throughout the book and will be prepared to try them out on your friends as games. For instance,

when you come to the first exercise on page 17, you can fill in all the adjectives that occur to you and then check your answers in the dictionary, or consult the Key to the Answers beginning on page 131.

6. If this procedure is followed with all the exercises throughout the book, you will have an accurate check on the progress you are making with your vocabulary-building.

This Key to the Answers appears in the regular trade edition only, not being included in the school edition for obvious reasons. These answers will prove useful when a dictionary is not handy and will make the book more usable as a game book for groups of people.

—THE PUBLISHERS.

I

Weary Words

A CHILD who can follow the adventures of Alice knows the meaning of many thousands of words; yet the sophisticated readers of novels are legion who, in spite of their extensive reading vocabularies, restrict themselves in their speaking and writing to a smaller vocabulary than Lewis Carroll's. Whether it is because of laziness or because of a fear of appearing "superior" (an inverse type of snobbishness), such people seldom range beyond words like *funny, scared, get, got, good, bad, also, mad, say, hope, come, go, ask, try, stand* (in the sense of *endure*), *start, better, worse, big, little, top, bottom, beginning, end, short, long, tall, bring, make, busy, keep, take* (require), *glad, sorry, like, hate, wrong, right, do, thing, fix, think, dumb, want* (wish), *see, mean* (adjective), *beat, pretty, real, give, take, strong, weak,* and a few hundred more. Such a limited speaking vocabulary, eked out by colloquialisms and the slang phrases of the moment, is sufficient to transmit immature thought in a childish and slovenly manner, but for the expression of mature thought with precision, discrimination, charm, and beauty such a vocabulary is clearly unserviceable.

It must be understood that there is nothing "wrong" with most of the words listed above. But to rely upon so limited a supply of words is to restrict the activity and the growth of the mind. One who finds everything in his life "good" — his automobile, the weather, his books (if any), his game of golf, his salary, his business, his food, his children, his friend, his wife — is indeed fortunate; but he is sadly undiscriminating. Such a possessor of good things, if he be an enthusiast, raises the expression of his satisfaction to a higher power by using such substitutes for "good" as *grand, wonderful, cute, nice, gorgeous, fine, lovely, slick, swell, splendid,* and *marvelous.* Legitimate, accurate, and otherwise desirable synonyms drawn from the great treasure-house of English words — synonyms which make his automobile powerful, economical, or reliable, the weather delightful, his books entertaining or instructive, his game of golf excellent, his salary ample, his business thriving, his food tasty or delectable, his children obedient, his friend loyal, and his wife faithful — seldom pass his lips.

And doubly cursed is the pessimist, the hypochondriac, the croaker; for not only does he have to dwell in the misery of his pessimism, but he experiences also the agony of imprisonment within the narrow bounds of such a vocabulary as *bad, awful, horrible, terrible, rotten, terrific,* and *fierce.* It is a miserable fate to have to look at life through dark blue glasses; it is worse to have no escape even into fresh and varied expressions of one's agony.

1 With the above remarks in mind, supply appropriate adjectives expressing approval of the following:

a tropic night
a football game
a pair of shoes
a suit of clothing
a child
a vacation
a department store
a cake of soap
a microscope
a poem
a moving picture
a policeman
an umpire
a dress
a statesman

advice
an actress
a boulevard
a popular tune
a typewriter
a sea trip
a waiter
a cigarette
a novel
a sermon
handwriting
a clown
a clergyman
an opera
a chair

a purchase on the stock market
the personality of a friend
the decision of a jury
the voice of a singer
the behavior of someone who
    has been defeated

2 Make a similar list of adjectives which express apposite disapproval of the persons and things suggested in section 1.

3 The word *thing* is of such wide applicability that it is seldom the accurate word; in your writing and formal speaking avoid it.

Improve the following sentences:

   (a) Put on all your things, for it is cold outside.
   (b) Bring your tennis things on Saturday.
   (c) It is an interesting thing to compare Hitler and Mussolini.
   (d) What is this thing on the dashboard?
   (e) He had a thing attached to his hat to keep it from blowing away.
   (f) The thing that prevents him from prospering is his poor judgment of men.
   (g) I have never seen such a big thing as the *Queen Mary*.
   (h) Jack wore a thing on his head to keep the sun out of his eyes.
   (i) This thing in the evening paper says that our national debt is increasing.
   (j) Wearing a monocle seems an affected thing to most Americans.
   (k) I have bought a thing to pull nails out with.

4 "It takes intelligence to choose the right word." In formal and literary English avoid the verb *to take* in the sense of to *require, need, want, demand, be necessary.*

Improve these sentences:

   (a) Business takes brains.
   (b) This lawn takes a great deal of care.
   (c) Powerful cars take a gallon of gasoline every eight or ten miles.
   (d) It takes intelligence to fly an airplane.

5 Perhaps your friend is not really clever or smart; perhaps you mean to say that he is intelligent, astute, intellectual, skillful, keen, acute, learned, well-informed, quick, sharp, sly, discerning, farsighted, perspicacious, wise, sagacious, dexterous, adroit, expert, deft, apt, proficient, efficient, skilled, capable, talented, artistic, workmanlike, profound, craftsmanlike, witty, amusing, keen-witted, jocular, waggish, funny, facetious, humorous, entertaining, ludicrous, diverting, or roguish.

What word best describes each of the following?

Napoleon	Einstein
Lincoln	an acrobat
Jefferson	a successful counterfeiter
Disraeli	Lewis Carroll
Shakespeare	an unobtrusive waiter
Groucho Marx	a successful card-sharper

a carpenter who has invented original short-cuts

6 Avoid the word *very*. Seldom do you really mean *very*, and when you do, it is well to seek an adjective or adverb that incorporates within itself the idea of *very*. A very attractive girl is more accurately captivating, charming, or fascinating; something very expensive is probably exorbitant; *very old* is *aged* or *ancient*; *very unwilling* is *loath*; *very active* is *agile* or *brisk* or *bustling* or *diligent*; *very lazy* is *indolent*; and *very afraid* is *terrified*, *terror-stricken*, or *appalled*.

Find single adjectives to express the following ideas:

(a) Very young, rich, poor, idle
(b) Very tired, short, silent, stupid
(c) Very steep, skillful, difficult, bright
(d) Very unusual, funny, dangerous, strong
(e) Very polite, plentiful, sad, happy
(f) Very pretty, patient, foolish, evil
(g) Very painful, stubborn, dark, neat
(h) Very mysterious, unhappy, quiet, wide
(i) Very kind, smooth, careful, wet
(j) Very late, deep, fast, dull
(k) Very willing, hopeful, proud, honest

7 *Get* is probably the most overused verb in the language but is often, in certain idioms, still a vigorous word. It is proper to speak of getting ahead in the world, getting the best of another person, getting under way, and the like; it is proper and desirable, in short, to use *get* when its use is deliberate and when it adds color or idiomatic vigor to language. But the indiscriminate use of *get* is a symptom of laziness. There is usually a more desirable word.

Improve the following sentences; or defend the use of *get*:.

(a) When you get to the library, get me a book.
(b) Get a cake of soap at the grocer's.
(c) We could get the house for only a year.
(d) We shall never get to our destination.
(e) He gets a thousand dollars a year in wages.

20

(f) They tried to get us to do them a favor.

(g) He got no profit from his business last year.

(h) We shall never get to the theatre on time.

(i) If you want to get rich, get up early.

(j) He gets tired easily.

(k) When they sang the sentimental old songs, he got sad.

(l) Our salesmen are not getting results.

(m) Get permission from your parents.

(n) The noise gets on my nerves.

(o) The moon is getting larger every day.

(p) As a child gets older, he gets a larger vocabulary, and as his vocabulary gets bigger, he gets a greater power of combining various ideas.

(q) Milton got famous by the publication of *Paradise Lost*, but he got little money for his work.

(r) Most newly married couples are eager to get a house in the suburbs.

(s) He gets a very small salary.

(t) The runner got put out at first base.

(u) Please get me a book from that shelf.

Fetch is a particularly useful word that is used too seldom. It combines the ideas of going to a place, obtaining some object, and returning with it to the starting point. Practice using it.

8 Find synonyms for *surprised*, in the popular sense of *astonished*. Improve upon the following sentences:

(a) He was surprised to hear that his sister had won the tennis tournament.

(b) If someone were to give me a million dollars, I should be surprised.

(c) He was so surprised at the news that he could not speak.

(d) Explain the following story:

It is said that on a certain occasion the wife of an English professor came unexpectedly upon him in the act of kissing the parlor-maid. She was naturally indignant.

"John!" she cried, "I am surprised at you."

"Pardon me, my dear," replied the professor meekly. "It is I who am surprised. You are merely astonished."

9 Instead of *want*, use *wish, desire, should like to, be desirous of, hope to, like, be eager to, prefer, fancy, care for, have a fancy for, be bent upon, covet, set one's heart upon, hunger for, hanker after, aspire to, sigh for, need, feel the want of, crave, long for.*

(a) Most men _____ fame.

(b) He _____ money for his vacation.

(c) I _____ your book collection.

(d) They _____ to keep out of the direct rays of the tropical sun.

(e) They _____ arrive in Singapore before the end of the month.

10 *Glad* and *sorry*: the general feeling of these words is often more precisely rendered by *pleased, happy, delighted, willing, content, overjoyed, satis-*

fied, and by *worried, displeased, distressed, upset, pained, concerned, chagrined, horrified, heartbroken, inconsolable, in despair, touched, penitent, repentant, apologetic, sad, contrite, conscience-stricken, regretful.*

Improve upon the following:

(a) He was glad to have our help.
(b) He was glad at the good fortune of his friend.
(c) I am glad that your father is feeling better.
(d) I shall be glad to let you drive my car.
(e) Most banks are glad to lend money to householders.
(f) I am sorry that I was so rude to you.
(g) Your mother seemed sorry that you had forgotten to call for her.
(h) Shelley was sorry about the death of Harriet.
(i) We said that we were sorry for our stupid mistake.
(j) You should be sorry for your sins.
(k) He was not sorry concerning his past life.
(l) Are you sorry to leave this charming house?

II

The Poisoned Well

THIS section concerns words which are frequently used with no respect for their proper meaning. To ignore the real meaning of a word and to ascribe to it another meaning is to poison the well of English words.

None of the following adjectives, as we have already seen in the foregoing chapter entitled "Weary Words," may be properly used in formal or literary English as adjectives of general and indiscriminate approval:

elegant	grand	swell	splendid	fine
nice	great	cute	wonderful	magnificent
gorgeous	slick	marvelous		

Each of these words has its proper meaning: *elegant* means tasteful and highly refined; *gorgeous* means ornate and richly colored. Use a dictionary to learn what the other words properly mean.

The case is the same with certain adjectives of general and vague disapproval: *awful, horrible, terrible, frightful, terrific, fierce.* These words are legitimate when they are associated with the expression of such feelings as genuine awe, horror, terror, fright, and the like. But a difficult examination is not awful; and a boring book is not terrific.

11 Consulting a dictionary, invent sentences in which each of the adjectives listed above (nineteen of them altogether) is properly used.

12 Improve the following sentences, or defend them as they now stand:

    (a) The party was grand because all the guests were nice and the dresses of the girls were magnificent.

    (b) The sunset was gorgeous; the prevailing color was red , but my eye was not nice enough to distinguish between the various shades.

    (c) Isn't it elegant that Harry won the first prize?

    (d) I know that you will not agree with me, but I think that her speech was wonderful.

13 The adverbs *awfully, horribly, terribly, frightfully,* and *terrifically* should not be used in the sense of *very.*

Improve the wording of the following sentences:

    (a) He is an awfully nice fellow, and his wife is swell; you will enjoy meeting them and seeing their baby, which is terribly cute.

    (b) It was terrifically hot in London.

    (c) She is frightfully nice.

14 In literary and formal English, if not elsewhere, avoid such colloquialisms as *tickled, dumb, mad,* and *mean* to denote *pleased, stupid, angry,* and *irritable.*

(a) It tickled me to death to see her so mad over a mere trifle.

(b) He is so dumb that he doesn't even know when somebody has been mean to him.

15 Avoid using the following words in the sense indicated:

funny   (meaning *odd*)   pretty (rather; "pretty old")
fix   (repair)   proposition (undertaking)
guess   (suppose)   party   (person)
balance (remainder)   *individual (person)*
claim   (assert)   fix   (difficulty: "in a fix")
couple (several)   ugly   (bad-tempered)
expect (suppose)
quite   (rather; *quite* means *entirely*)

16 Correct or improve upon the following sentences:

(a) I guess you think Tom is awfully nice, but we have had more experience with him than you, and consequently we think he is terribly mean.

(b) The etchings of Whistler are grand, but those of Rembrandt, though often very dark, are gorgeous.

(c) I guess that such a skillful mechanic can fix the car in a few minutes, but most garage men would take a whole day.

---

* *Individual* should be used in the sense of *person* only when one wishes to separate the individual from a group; e.g., The team as a whole was poor, but the individuals were nearly all above the average.

(d) I asked Mr. Jackson for a raise in salary, but he claimed the firm could not afford to advance the salaries of any of its employees.

(e) The San Francisco-Oakland bridge was a difficult proposition.

17 Avoid these words in the senses indicated:

literally (actually)
humans (human beings)
way   (in such a phrase as "way ahead")
against   (in the sense of "opposed to")
start to (begin to)
so   (therefore)
figure   (as a verb meaning "believe")
around   (meaning "about")

18 Improve the following sentences:

(a) We figure that if we had caught hold of the rope as he fell overboard, he would have had a pretty good chance of being saved.

(b) She literally swept the room with her eyes.

(c) Humans can get way ahead of others in life if they will start at an early age to make friends with important individuals.

(d) I am against any tampering with the laws of this country, so I am joining the Anti-New-Law Association, an organization of around ten thousand members that has already proved itself powerful.

III

Synonyms

Two or more words having the same or approximately the same meaning but differing in emphasis, suggestion, or usage are called synonyms. *Rich, wealthy, opulent, moneyed, affluent, well-to-do,* and *well off* are synonyms; and so are *big, large, tremendous, enormous, great, huge, immense, titanic, vast, gigantic, monstrous,* and *colossal.*

At first glance these adjectives may seem to differ little in meaning, but a moment of thought will show that no two of the synonyms have precisely the same connotation. It is obvious, for instance, that one who is opulent is much wealthier than one who is well off; that an acorn may be big or large but hardly titanic; that a book may be huge but hardly vast; and that a human eye may be large but, excepting in the head of a mythical giant, scarcely monstrous.

To collect lists of synonyms and to distinguish their meanings is one effective way to enlarge the vocabulary. Consider for a moment some of the synonyms of *old: olden, hoary, antique, antiquated, aged, senile, time-honored, ancient, decrepit, patriarchal, elderly, venerable, time-worn, primitive, aboriginal, antediluvian, prehistoric,* and *passé.* Try to decide which of these words denotes the greatest age; surely it is not *elderly* or *passé*. Is it *ancient, antediluvian,* or *prehistoric?* Determine also which synonym denotes the least age; and then using the two selected synonyms as the top and bottom words of a vertical list, arrange the rest of the words between them in descending order.

In your attempt to make such a list you will encounter difficulties. You will notice, for instance, that some of the adjectives are used to describe only persons: a man can be called senile, but not a bicycle or a building. On the other hand, a piece of paper, no matter how old, can hardly be described as decrepit. The difficulty may be resolved by making two lists of words, one list containing adjectives applicable to people and living creatures, and another of those which apply only to things. Some of the words, you will find, appear in both lists. If a word such as *olden* does not seem to be used to describe either people or things, consider in what connection it generally is used.

When you make lists of synonyms, ask yourself such questions as these; for the purposes of illustration we shall continue with the synonyms of *old*:

(a) Does *decrepit* have any suggestion other than that of advanced age? (The answer is that *decrepit* suggests a considerable physical breakdown which has accompanied the coming of age. One can refer to a tottery old man as "decrepit" but not to an old man who is in excellent physical condition.)

(b) What about *remote?* Is it applicable to persons and things? To events? To times and places?

(c) Can the Nile River properly be termed hoary? antiquated? senile? venerable? passé?

(d) Which word applies most fittingly to an outmoded style: *olden, aboriginal, passé?*

(e) Are any of the words ever used humorously or facetiously? What does *superannuated* mean, and how is it used?

19 Collect synonyms of *new.* Do there appear to be so many as there are of *old?* (Try to explain why.) The explanation is not difficult.

Arrange the synonyms of *new* in order between the two extremes of the list.

20 Collect synonyms of *happy* and arrange a list in descending order, placing at the head of your list the adjective which suggests the greatest degree of happiness.

21 Proceed in the same way with the synonyms of *large;* of *small.*

22 Distinguish in meaning and usage between *trip, journey, tour, voyage, excursion, flight, pilgrimage, expedition, jaunt, circuit, ramble, outing.*

(a) Which are short? Which long?
(b) Which have definite goals or objectives?
(c) Which are aimless, purposeless?
(d) Which can take place on water? Which on land?

(e) Which can take place only on water? Only on land?

(f) Which can be accomplished only on foot?

(g) Is there any kind of travel which can be accomplished only by airplane?

23 *Fragrance, fetor, smell, odor, aroma, redolence, stench, stink, perfume, bouquet, scent, fetidness.*

(a) Which of these words denote pleasant nasal sensations? Which unpleasant?

(b) Are any of these words general in meaning, not restricting themselves to either pleasant or offensive odors?

(c) Which of the words denotes the most pleasant sensation? Which the most unpleasant?

(d) Is any of the words so undignified that you would not use it in a drawing room or in making a speech to a cultivated audience?

24 Make a list of at least ten adjectives synonymous with *pretty*. Arrange them in order according to the degrees of prettiness which they express, placing first in the list the word which denotes the greatest beauty. Use each of the words in a sentence. Try to invent sentences in which some of the synonyms could not reasonably be substituted for the adjective which you have used. The following questions will give you some hints how to proceed:

(a) Can an automobile be considered comely, a building personable, or a house well-favored?

31

(b) Is a sunset best described as beautiful, beauteous, or handsome?

(c) Are roses beautiful, good-looking, pretty, sightly, or attractive?

25 Find as many synonyms as you can for each of the adjectives in the list which follows. In each case determine the two synonyms which represent the extremes of the quality described by the adjective, and list the other synonyms in orderly sequence between those extremes: *ugly, stingy, neat, timid, brave, polite, soft, hard, careful, little, far, heavy, strong, weak,* and *imprudent.*

26 Consider the following verbs of motion: *move, go, pass, shift, slide, glide, flow, run, drift, stream, wander, sweep along, speed, walk, march, step along, pace, plod, trudge, tramp, stalk, stride, toddle, jog on, make one's way, coast, skim, skate, shuffle, scurry, scuttle.*

(a) Which of these words pertain only to motion on foot?

(b) Which imply the greatest speed? Which the least?

(c) What words are general in their suggestion of motion, without implications of the means?

(d) Consider the habitual movements of a dirigible, a horse, an automobile, a rowboat, a bullet, a current of air, a runner, and a shadow. Which verbs apply best to each?

27 Make a list of verbs which might properly be substituted for *say;* a few of them are *assert, affirm, declare, state, protest, profess, allege, maintain, announce, aver, swear, speak, utter, breathe, whisper, murmur, declaim, cry, shout, mutter, roar, yell,* and *moan.* There are many more. Make a practice in speaking and writing of using synonyms for *say.*

28 *Endeavor, strive, try, undertake, attempt, essay*

(a) When one tries to achieve something, does he try so hard as when he endeavors?

(b) Would you try to sharpen a pencil, or endeavor to do it? Why? Are there any circumstances under which one might strive to sharpen a pencil?

(c) How strenuously does one try when he essays to do something?

(d) Which implies the exertion of greater energy, *to strive* or *to attempt?*

(e) Which word implies a greater prospect of success than the others?

(f) Use each word in a sentence designed to illustrate the peculiar implications of that word.

29 *Conquer, overcome, subject, beat, crush, worst, win, checkmate, defeat, quell, prevail over, subjugate, surmount, vanquish, subdue, overthrow, overpower, down, humble, overmaster, master, put down, rout.*

33

Supply appropriate verbs in the blank spaces:

(a) Because of its spirit the team was never
_____ even when it was _____.

(b) One would not speak of _____ing an
opponent at checkers.

(c) My friend _____ all his competitors in
the oratorical contest by his vivid description of how Richard II _____ the
rebellion of Wat Tyler.

(d) A defeated army, marching away from the
scene of battle in good order, cannot be
described as having been _____.

30 Make a list of nouns that represent beings pos-
sessed of magical or supernatural power, such as *sorcerer* and *witch*. Distinguish between them as to their
meaning and as to the particular powers which accompany each.

31 *Let, permit, give permission, allow, bear with,
tolerate, suffer, grant, concede, assent, acquiesce, agree
to, accord, vouchsafe, favor, indulge, privilege, author-
ize, sanction, warrant, give carte blanche to, consent
to, brook, put up with, submit to, undergo, support,
abide.*

Some of these words imply a degree of willingness on
the part of the person giving permission, but others
imply reluctance and even definite dislike.

(a) What is the difference between letting a person drive one's automobile, and tolerating, suffering, agreeing to, authorizing, and vouchsafing such a privilege?

(b) Use each of the verbs in a sentence of your own composition, and experiment in substituting various synonyms. As you do so, take note of changes in meaning, and be on the alert for nonsensical and unidiomatic combinations.

(c) Which of the words imply superiority on the part of the person giving permission? Which suggest that he is the underdog?

32 You will need to refer constantly to a dictionary to answer the following questions. The larger the dictionary, the better; Webster's *New International Dictionary* or Funk and Wagnall's *New Standard Dictionary* in their unabridged form will serve you equally well.

(a) What is the difference between humor and wit?

(b) A plan and a scheme?

(c) An instrument and a tool?

(d) A shop and a store?

(e) Advice and counsel?

(f) A trophy, a memento, and a souvenir?

(g) A prison and a jail?

(h) Pilfering, thieving, stealing, purloining, and appropriating?

(i) Love, liking, and affection?

(j) *Ridiculous, funny, laughable, silly,* and *absurd?*

(k) Is a good pun humor or wit?

(l) Would a clergyman speak of a plan or a scheme to raise money for building a new church? Is there a still more dignified word that he might use?

(m) Would you care to have a surgeon operate upon you with a surgical tool? Why not?

(n) Is there more stigma attached to having been in prison or in jail?

(o) Can one properly be described as pilfering a million dollars?

(p) When a well-dressed man slips on a banana-peel, does it strike you at first as absurd, ridiculous, funny, laughable, or silly? If you had to make the choice, would you rather have people consider you funny or laughable?

33 There are a dozen or more words that denote brief existence: *temporary, short, fugitive, fleeting, transient, ephemeral, evanescent, flying, momentary, passing, flitting, transitory, brief, short-lived,* and *impermanent.*

(a) What word applies most accurately to lightning?

(b) To the life of a butterfly?

(c) To a popular but worthless book?

(d) To a glance?

(e) To the iridescence of silk or oil?

(f) To one's hesitation in the making of a decision?

(g) To a sudden headache which lasts only five minutes?

(h) To an automobile which wears out in two years of ordinary service?

SYNONYMS

34 There are twenty or more words that denote the contrary of *brief*: *never-ending, perennial, undying, eternal, deathless, imperishable, endless, everlasting, perpetual, without end, unfailing, unceasing, ever-living, unfading, fadeless, immortal, interminable, timeless, unending, continual, ceaseless, incessant.*

(a) Which of the above words suggests the absence of either beginning or end?

(b) How many of these adjectives could properly apply to the fame of Abraham Lincoln? Why would *timeless* be improper in that context? What other words would be inapplicable? Why?

(c) Which of the words would be out of place in reference to an irritating sound which never ceases?

(d) Is there one of the words which implies annoyance on the part of the speaker?

(e) Which word would best describe a steady rain which apparently will never come to an end?

(f) Which lasts longer, something perennial or something undying?

35 *Knave, rogue, villain, rascal, blackguard, bad man, wrongdoer, evildoer, sinner, transgressor, scoundrel, miscreant, caitiff, wretch, reptile, viper, serpent, roué, rake, rough, rowdy, ruffian, hoodlum, culprit, criminal, malefactor, felon, riffraff, curmudgeon, ras-*

callion, sneak, scamp, good-for-nothing, reprobate, scalawag, rapscallion, etc., etc.

If we must call names, let us at least not be so carried away by our indignation or anger that we forget the immense vocabulary of insulting words which the English language puts at our disposal. Some of the words are jocular, some stern, some vigorously derogatory, some aloof and cool. Study them.

36 *Imitate, copy, take off, mimic, ape, simulate, personate, reproduce, repeat, parallel, borrow from, counterfeit, parody, forge, burlesque, travesty, follow, emulate.*

Study the words in the above list, and fill each space in the following sentences with the word that best fits the context.

(a) Garrick often _____ed Dr. Johnson for the amusement of his friends, but he could only hope to _____ the character of that great man.

(b) To _____ another is to flatter him.

(c) Art _____s nature.

(d) To _____ another's handwriting is not necessarily to forge it.

(e) In his dress and voice he _____s his betters.

(f) What is the difference between the verbs *to parody, to burlesque,* and *to travesty?*

37 In the following list, some of the words are synonymous with (1) *enthusiasm*, (2) *imagination*, (3) *impudence*, (4) *name*, (5) *mob*, and (6) *necessity*. Put the suitable number before each word.

Ardor, effrontery, zeal, pertness, ecstasy, forwardness, rudeness, excitement, title, fanaticism, phantasy, fervency, rapture, fancy, impertinence, fervor, incivility, cognomen, canaille, exigency, extremity, insolence, frenzy, epithet, rabble, transport, inspiration, populace, requisite, passion, urgency.

38 Name as many different kinds of vehicles as you can think of. Your list should be large; Roget in his *Thesaurus of English Words and Phrases* includes some two hundred terms in his list. You should be able to find at least twenty-five. Remember to include the following categories:

(a) vehicles which carry people
(b) vehicles which carry materials
(c) horse-drawn vehicles
(d) motor-driven vehicles
(e) vehicles drawn by animals other than horses
(f) vehicles for use solely on ice
(g) vehicles with fewer than four wheels
(h) vehicles used only on railroads

IV

Antonyms

An antonym is just the opposite of a synonym; that is, an antonym is a word expressing an idea directly opposite to that of another word. *Friend* and *enemy* are antonyms; so are *good* and *bad*, *large* and *small*, *early* and *late*, *saint* and *sinner*, and *come* and *go*.

Be as accurate as possible in finding the exact antonym in each case. *Tiny*, for instance, is not the precise antonym of *large* because *tiny* indicates a greater degree of smallness than *large* does of largeness. *Small* corresponds more closely to *large* in the degree of size which it denotes; and *huge* or *enormous* serves better as the precise antonym of *tiny*.

Some words have no exact antonyms. There are no antonyms at all for nouns like *sorcerer*, *lawyer*, and *advice*; for such adjectives as *weird*, *favorite*, *exquisite*, and *astounding*; and for such verbs as *negotiate*, *drench*, *hoot*, and *spell*. Is there an antonym of *middle*? *End* will not do, for *end* is the antonym of *beginning*.

39 Find antonyms for the following adjectives: *happy*, *skillful*, *beautiful*, *ignorant*, *hurried*, and *imminent*.

40 What are the precise antonyms of *discouraged, tired, absurd, voluntary, obvious, admirable?*

41 What are the most accurate antonyms of *candid, mountain, benevolent, forceful,* and *wholesome?*

42 Do any of the following words have corresponding words of precisely opposite meaning: *blemish, conspiracy, caricature, eye, hoop, pencil?*

43 Find antonyms for these words: *fool, faultless, property, dapper, senator, co-operate, rival.* If you cannot find a precise antonym for any of these words, try to explain to yourself why the antonym is lacking from the English language. There is always a good reason. *Hat,* for instance, has no precise antonym because there is no object in existence concerned with covering the head which does *not* cover the head! *Shoe* is not a true antonym of *hat;* it is scarcely more satisfactory as an antonym than *glove,* or *coat,* or *collar,* or *dress.*

44 *Combination, copy, sequence, dispersion, plurality, irregularity, continuance, paternity, energy, interval, support, distortion, impulse, gravity,* and *motion.*

From the list of nouns which follows, choose words that are antonyms of each of the nouns in the list above:

filament	smallness	redness
amorphism	synchronism	fraction
recall	pendency	decomposition
intempestivity	repetition	periodicity
recoil	originality	assemblage
reversion	preterition	quiescence
continuity	precedence	anachronism
posterity	prototype	cessation
vision	symmetry	levity
agriculture	contiguity	inelasticity

45 Which of the following words is the most precise antonym of (a) drudgery, (b) facetiousness, and (c) prudence?

ease	dullness	indiscretion
idleness	gravity	thoughtlessness
relaxation	seriousness	indolence
repose	sobriety	wastefulness
solemnity	stupidity	temerity
stolidity	folly	rashness

46 Which of the following words appear to have no antonyms; what explanation can you give of this deficiency?

commerce	encouraging	collision
crew	revelry	duty
harness	circumference	pecuniary
bold	property	round
knight	prevent	January

47 Find one antonym for each of the following nouns:

adversity	oblivion	condemnation
loss	truth	jealousy
receipt	shortcoming	ambush
seclusion	plunge	summit
contempt	orthodoxy	holy

48 Find one antonym for each of the following adjectives:

foolish	pensive	proficient
latent	idiotic	secure
permanent	professional	indefensible
stable	professorial	tenacious
sullen	taciturn	liberal
deep	extemporaneous	favorite
sensual	significant	

49 Find antonyms for each of the following verbs:

regret	condense	possess	humiliate
believe	deplore	amuse	glower
aspire	withdraw	shout	praise
serve	hum	ingratiate	bless
hurtle	dawn	sicken	glorify
degenerate	cure	speed	stagger
		anger	

50 Find an antonym for each of the following nouns:

fame	erudition	squalor
thoroughfare	rectitude	veracity
circumspection	chaos	innuendo
taciturnity	scholar	axiom
mercy	docility	flattery

51 Find an antonym for each of these adjectives:

restive	eager	rebellious	fictitious
tentative	lewd	reluctant	bizarre
propitious	auxiliary	prejudiced	precarious
deficient	physical	fractious	native

52 Collect antonyms of

teach	fail	gain
quit	obey	give
warn	permit	lend
attack	offer	hope
defend	promise	confess

53 Collect antonyms of

learn	disobey	sell
persevere	forbid	borrow
tempt	refuse	receive
reject	deny	keep
succeed	lose	laugh

54 Collect four synonyms and four antonyms for each of the following verbs:

go forward
go up
arrive
appear

ask
remember
amuse
conceal

55 Find five synonyms and five antonyms for each of these verbs:

dislike
take
open
win
praise
help

begin
labor
live
join
fall
eat

56 Make lists of synonyms and of antonyms for each of these adjectives:

wrong
smooth
generous
first
young

slow
soft
wide
alike
empty

sweet
thick
stupid
wet
loud

short
open
sad
difficult
optimistic

57 Make lists of synonyms and antonyms for each of the following nouns:

beginning	top	wisdom	war
man	care	friend	cause
knowledge	warning	life	sound
danger	youth	outside	health
front	pleasure	good	master

58 Collect synonyms and antonyms for the following adjectives:

short	heavy	dark	clear
sharp	lazy	cheap	important
enough	sane	free	convex
possible	useful	curved	willing
clean	high	plain	visible
strong	hot	loud	true

V

Definitions

IN PREVIOUS sections of this book we have dealt chiefly with ways of building the passive vocabulary — the reading vocabulary. One of the best methods of building the active vocabulary — words which come readily to the lips when one tries to express a thought of more than ordinary difficulty — is to exercise oneself in the making of definitions.

What, for instance, is an assassin? Consider the value of the following definition: "An assassin is a man who kills another man." Obviously that definition is unsatisfactory; for under its terms the assassin may be the driver of an automobile who by accident kills another, and furthermore, to judge by the definition, the assassin must be a male adult who kills another male adult.

Let us try again: "An assassin is a person who murders someone else." On examination this definition also proves unsatisfactory. Are all murderers assassins? Is it necessary to succeed in the assassination in order to be termed an assassin, or is one an assassin if he merely undertakes the murder?

Again: "An assassin is one who treacherously, and often for hire, undertakes to kill another." Study that definition and try to improve upon it; then consult an unabridged dictionary and compare your definition.

59 *Table*: compare the following definitions made by students, choose the best, and tell precisely why it is superior to the others.

(a) A table is a surface with four legs attached at the corners and designed to hold small objects such as cigarette trays, vases, and dishes.

(b) A table is a wooden article with several legs and possibly a small drawer whose top consists of a flat surface on which small objects may be laid.

(c) A table is a piece of furniture of a height convenient to human beings; it has one or more legs supporting a flat surface on which various articles may be placed for human uses of various kinds.

(d) A table consists of a wooden surface supported by wooden supports (called legs); the legs are tall enough to hold the surface about four feet above the ground.

(e) A table is a piece of furniture made of any kind of material at all; you are not supposed to sit on it, but people sometimes do; usually meals are served at a table.

Now make your own definition of a table; compare your finished definition with that in an unabridged dictionary.

DEFINITIONS

60 The old trick of asking someone to define a circular staircase, hoping that he will resort to the use of his hands, should at this point be played on oneself. What is a circular staircase?

N. B. When you make a definition, you must be sure that the definition does not contain the word itself or a word closely connected with it. Neither is it satisfactory to give a mere synonym as a definition. To say that *beautiful* means "possessing beauty" or that *plump* means "fat" is not to make a full and accurate definition.

61 Define the following:

- (a) a friend
- (b) a wheelbarrow
- (c) an automobile
- (d) a clergyman
- (e) a book
- (f) a prejudice

62 Define the following verbs:

- (a) to boil
- (b) to laugh
- (c) to run
- (d) to walk
- (e) to gamble
- (f) to yawn
- (g) to ascertain

63 Define the following adjectives:

(a) zigzag
(b) beautiful
(c) plump
(d) early
(e) disgusting
(f) sporadic
(g) continual

64 Define the following verbs:

(a) to trot
(b) to expostulate
(c) to remonstrate
(d) to wrestle
(e) to vote
(f) to listen
(g) to hope

65 Define the following nouns:

(a) bog
(b) school
(c) sky
(d) king
(e) wharf

DEFINITIONS

66 Define the following nouns:

(a) dog
(b) floor
(c) door
(d) yacht
(e) shovel

67 Define the following nouns:

(a) bicycle
(b) knee
(c) murder
(d) pyramid
(e) triangle
(f) embarrassment

68 Criticise the following definitions and try to make better ones:

(a) *Saddle:* a sort of chair without arms in which one sits when he rides a horse.
(b) *Indescribable:* not capable of being described.
(c) *Oval:* almost round but fatter at one end than the other.
(d) *Gentleman:* a man who has clean fingernails and who speaks pleasantly to everyone.
(e) *Relic:* something left over to the modern day from an event that happened long ago.
(f) *Square:* having four corners and four equal sides.

(g) *Sickly:* not sick quite yet, but about to be.

(h) *Pink:* the color of human fingernails.

(i) *Solemn:* calculated to impresss one with a sense of dignity.

(j) *Banquet:* an important dinner after which people smoke cigars and listen to many speakers.

(k) *Fish:* an animal that swims in the water.

(l) *Smile:* to contort the face in the vicinity of the mouth and the eyes in order to convey the impression that one is amused or pleasant.

VI

Malapropisms
or
What Did She Mean?

IN SHERIDAN's comedy, *The Rivals*, there is a famous female named Mrs. Malaprop, a pretentious old creature who is remarkable for her ability to misapply long words. She urges Lydia, for instance, to illiterate her lover from her memory; and on another occasion she maintains that Lydia is as headstrong as an allegory on the banks of the Nile.

Just as Mrs. Malaprop mistook *illiterate* for *obliterate*, and *allegory* for *alligator*, so writers and speakers sometimes mistake the meanings of such words as *desirous, portends, incredulous,* and *humility;* to their way of thinking, an automobile is desirous rather than desirable, a man portends rather than pretends to be sincere, someone's stupidity is incredulous rather than incredible, and an unfortunate experience is not a humiliation but a humility. Such errors have come to be known as Malapropisms.

69 The following sentences contain Malapropisms drawn from *The Rivals*. The Malapropisms are italicized; in the case of each of her mistakes substitute the word that Mrs. Malaprop meant to use.

(a) Now don't attempt to *extirpate* yourself from the matter; you know I have proof *controvertible* of it.

(b) Nay, nay, Sir Anthony, you are an absolute *misanthropy*. (She means "a hater of mankind.")

(c) I would by no means wish a daughter of mine to be a *progeny*.

(d) I would have her instructed in *geometry*, that she might know something of the *contagious* countries.

(e) She should be a mistress of *orthodoxy*, that she might not misspell and mispronounce words so shamefully as girls usually do.

(f) (After having laid down a full program for the education of a young woman) This is what I would have a young woman know; — and I don't think there is a *superstitious* article in it.

(g) If ever you betray what you are entrusted with, you forfeit my *malevolence* forever.

(h) Few gentlemen now-a-days know how to value the *ineffectual* qualities in a woman; few think how little knowledge becomes a gentlewoman.

(i) I have since laid Sir Anthony's *preposition* before her.

(j) This very day I have *interceded* another letter from the fellow.

(k) My *affluence* over my niece is very small.

70 Here are ten more sentences with Malapropisms prominently displayed. Correct these sentences as suggested in the preceding exercise.

(a) I should say nothing to your friend about the matter for fear that words may *participate* a quarrel.

(b) When you return from Europe I want you to be sure to tell me the *perpendiculars* of your trip.

(c) The sinking of a great liner at sea is almost always a tragic *antistrophe*.

(d) The *comparison* of King Arthur's horse was richly decked with gold and diamonds.

(e) I have never before met such a childish man; he was as innocent and *ingenious* as a baby.

(f) What is the cost of a year's *intuition* at Harvard University?

(g) He will be twenty-one years old in February and consequently will be *illegible* for the baseball team.

(h) If you were to experience a pleasure so great that you could not describe it, you would speak of that pleasure as being *infallible*.

(i) Sometimes an apparently trivial event will have serious *imprecations*.

71 Detect the Malapropisms in the following sentences and correct them:

(a) His actions are contemptuous because they are dishonest.

(b) Whistler's skill as an etcher was masterful.

(c) Any honorable gentleman must depreciate such contemptible conduct as George MacPherson's.

(d) A loyal soldier has no alternate but to go forward when he is ordered.

(e) It is a regretful circumstance that great writers like Samuel Johnson often have to pass much of their life in poverty.

(f) He was always headstrong and precipitous in his actions.

(g) The burglar made a forceful entry into the clergyman's house.

(h) The undergrowth in the tropics is luxurious by reason of the combined dampness and heat.

(i) Because of his intelligence and charm, I predicate for him a brilliant future.

(j) Precede straight along this street until you come to the third traffic light; then turn to the left and you will find yourself on the road to New York.

(k) I have tried to tantalize his character, but there are several elements in it which I do not understand.

(l) He was elected to the legislation only last year, and since his term is for six years, he cannot take a trip round the world for some time.

VII

Word Derivation: Latin

THE source of a large part of our English vocabulary is Latin. Thousands of Latin words, coming direct into English or passing through the French language, have enriched our basically Teutonic tongue with a variety and resourcefulness of vocabulary unrivaled in any other language.

Latin is a slighted subject in a great many American schools and universities. This section of *Twelve Ways to Build a Vocabulary* may consequently seem strange, formidable, and even repellent to some students, but it is of extraordinary importance. Some knowledge of Latin, if only of the meaning of a few hundred words, is indispensable if one is to feel at ease with the English language as an instrument of thought. A knowledge, for instance, of the Latin word *acer*, meaning "sharp," will put one on easy terms with the familiar English words *acerbity*, *acrid*, and *acrimony*, and with the less familiar *exacerbate*. A consciousness that the Latin *aequus* means "equal," facilitates the adoption into one's vocabulary of *equanimity*, *equilibrium*, *equinox*, *equity*, *equivocal*, and *equation*.

By way of practice, remembering that each of the

following words contains the idea of *love*, discover what each word means. Use a dictionary freely.

amatory	amenity	amicable
amity	amorous	enamor

Investigate also the meanings of *animadvert*, *animosity*, *equanimity*, *magnanimous*, and *pusillanimous* and learn what essential idea is common to all of these words.

72 Learn the following Latin words and roots:

annus — year	*cantare* — to sing
cadere — to fall	*carn* — flesh
caedere — to cut	*catena* — chain
calere — to be hot	*centum* — one hundred
candere — to shine	*crescere* — to grow

What are the meanings of the following words:

(a) annual, biennial, triennial, perennial, annals, superannuate
(b) cadence, decadence, deciduous, occident
(c) caesura, excision
(d) nonchalant, caloric, calories
(e) candor, candid, incandescent, candidate, incendiary
(f) canorous, canticle, canto, enchant, incantation, precentor
(g) carnal, carnivorous, incarnation
(h) concatenation, catenary

(i) centenary, centennial, centigrade, centipede, centurion

(j) crescent, excrescence, increment, decrement

73 Learn the following Latin words and their meanings:

cubare — to lie down
cura — care
decem — ten
dicere — to say
ducere — to lead

iungere — to join
legare — to send
nasci — to be born (past participal — natus)
nocere — to hurt
nomen — name

What are the meanings of the following English words? How is the meaning of each word related to the meaning of the Latin word from which it is derived?

(a) cubicle, incubate, incubus
(b) accurate, curate, procurator, secure, sinecure
(c) decemvir, decennial, decimate, decade
(d) edict, indict (pronounced "indite")
(e) educate, induce, superinduce, duchess, conduce
(f) conjugal, junta
(g) delegate, relegate
(h) agnate, cognate, innate, nascent, natal
(i) innocuous, noxious, obnoxious
(j) cognomen, ignominy, nomenclature, nominal, synonym

74 Learn the meanings of the following Latin words:

quattuor — four	*verus* — true
rapere — to seize	*vestis* — clothing
venire — to come	*via* — a way

What are the meanings of the following English words? What other words can you think of that come from the same Latin sources?

(a) quadrant, quadruped, quadrille, quarantine, squadron
(b) rapacious, rapine, ravish
(c) contravene, convene, intervene, supervene
(d) aver, veracious, verify, verity, verisimilitude
(e) transvestite, divest, vestment, vestry
(f) deviate, obviate, pervious, impervious, viaduct

75 What basic meaning underlies the words in each of the following groups?

(a) aquatic, aquarium, aqueduct, aqueous, subaqueous
(b) asperity, exasperate
(c) audible, audience, auditory
(d) auction, augment, august, author
(e) aureate, oriel, oriflamme, oriole, ormulu

76 With the help of a dictionary, answer the following questions:

(a) What similarity of idea is there in *capital, decapitation, capitulate, occiput,* and *sinciput.*

(b) How does the idea of "cross" enter into each of the following words: *crucial*, *crucify*, *cruciform*, *excruciate*?

(c) Judging from the meanings of *culpable*, *culprit*, and *exculpate*, what does the Latin word *culpa* mean?

77 Know the meaning of each of the following words, and keep in mind the basic meaning which is common to all the words in each group:

(a) acclivity, declivity, proclivity
(b) collet, colporteur, decollation
(c) cornea, corn, cornet, cornucopia, unicorn
(d) corps, corpse, corpulent, corpuscle, incorporate
(e) credible, miscreant, recreant

78 Think of English words containing the following Latin words:

dominus, a lord
durus, hard
errare, to stray
exter-, outer

fides, faith
flagrare, to burn
fluere, to flow
facilis, easy

Be sure to include *dominion*, *duress*, *obdurate*, *aberration*, *extraneous*, *diffident*, *perfidious*, *flagrant*, and *influx*.

79 What is the meaning that is common to *gregarious*, *egregious*, *congregate*, *aggregate*, and *segregate*?

What does each of these words mean? Use each in a sentence.

80 Learn the meanings of the following words, and notice the basic meaning which obtains throughout each group:

    (a) alleviate, leaven, levity (*levis*, light)

    (b) illicit, licentious, licentiate (*licere*, to be allowable)

    (c) obliterate, alliteration, literal (*litera*, a letter)

    (d) elongate, longevity, longitude (*longus*, long)

    (e) loquacity, obloquy, ventriloquist, soliloquy, colloquy (*loqui*, to speak)

    (f) elucidate, pellucid (*lucere*, to shine)

    (g) malapert, malinger, malversation (*malus*, bad)

    (h) amanuensis, manacle, manipulate, manual, manumit, manuscript, manufacture (*manus*, hand)

    (i) mediate, medial, medieval, mediocre (*medius*, middle)

81 What meaning is common to the words in the following groups? What does each word mean?

    (a) complacent, placable, placid

    (b) esplanade, pianoforte, plane

    (c) complement, expletive, plenary, plenitude

    (d) complicity, explicit, supplicate

    (e) deprecate, imprecate, precarious

(f) primeval, primogeniture, primrose
(g) approbation, probity
(h) impugn, oppugn, pugnacity
(i) desecrate, sacerdotal, sacrilege, sacrament, execrate.

82 Trace the following words back to their Latin roots, and as an aid in remembering their meanings, observe how the Latin meaning lingers in the modern word. Make free use of a large dictionary.

(a) desultory, resilient, saltation
(b) salubrious, salutary
(c) satiate, saturate
(d) prescience, sciolist
(e) escutcheon, scutiform
(f) bisect, insect, intersect
(g) assiduous, insidious
(h) disseminate, seminary
(i) obsequies, obsequious
(j) assimilate, dissimulate, simulate
(k) sonorous, resonant
(l) astringent, stringent
(m) entablature
(n) contiguous, tangible

83 Deal with the following words as you did with those in section 82:

(a) tegument
(b) contemporaneous, extempore

(c) tenacious, pertinacity
(d) attenuate, extenuate
(e) attrition, trite
(f) distort, tort, tortuous, torque
(g) trireme, triumvir, triglyph
(h) tumulus, tumid, intumescent
(i) inundation, undulate
(j) valediction, valetudinarian
(k) divaricate, prevaricate
(l) convivial, vivacity, vivisection
(m) avocation, evoke, revoke, vociferous

For other Latin elements in the English vocabulary, see section XII, which deals with prefixes.

VIII

Word Derivation: Doub⌐

AN INTERESTING approach to the study of word derivation is by way of doublets. A doublet is a pair of words both of which derive ultimately from the same source, but each differs from the other in meaning, usage, or form. *Abridge* and *abbreviate*, for instance, are doublets. Each comes from the Latin *abbreviare*, meaning to shorten; but their use in English and their forms are obviously different.

Like *abbreviate* and *abridge*, many doublets are ultimately of Latin origin, but one of the pair has usually come into English direct from the Latin and preserves an unmistakable resemblance to the Latin word; whereas the other has often passed through the French language on its way into English and has taken on changes of pronunciation and spelling which sometimes make the word almost unrecognizable as an offspring of the parent word.

Consider the following pairs of doublets from the points of view of their mutual origins and of their present meanings:

84

    (a) aggrieve, aggravate
    (b) amiable, amicable

(c) announce annunciate
(d) appraise, appreciate
(e) assemble assimilate

85

(a) benison, benediction
(b) camera, chamber
(c) complaisant, complacent
(d) comprehend, comprise
(e) confound, confuse

86

(a) construe, construct
(b) crevice, crevasse
(c) fend, defend
(d) diurnal, journal
(e) envious, invidious

87

(a) inept, inapt
(b) indict, indite
(c) invoke, invocate
(d) malediction, malison
(e) maxim, maximum

88

(a) mentor, monitor
(b) metal, mettle
(c) mobile, movable
(d) obedience, obeisance
(e) parole, palaver

89

(a) penance, penitence

(b) plaintiff, plaintive
(c) poignant, pungent
(d) potent, puissant
(e) priest, presbyter
(f) ransom, redemption
(g) reconnaissance, recognizance
(h) reprieve, reprove
(i) sacristan, sexton
(j) assess, assize

90

(a) lasso, lace
(b) dainty, dignity
(c) guest, hostile
(d) shirt, skirt
(e) lien, ligament
(f) reason, ration
(g) gentile, genteel
(h) cordial, hearty
(i) tavern, tabernacle
(j) cancer, canker

91

(a) What distinction is there between a benison and a benediction?
(b) What is the difference between a·valet and a varlet?
(c) What is the difference between a wrack and a wreck?

92

(a) Is a crevasse a kind of crevice? Which word is limited in its application? To what?

(b) Who is the more bewildered, one who is confused or one who is confounded?

(c) What function does a monitor perform that a mentor does not? Is there any real distinction between the two words?

(d) Of *penitence* and *penance*, one is synonymous with punishment. Which?

(e) Can an odor be called both pungent and poignant at the same time? What is the difference?

(f) Both a sacristan and a sexton hold offices connected with a church. Which office is of the greater dignity? What are the duties of each?

(g) If one has been arrested, is he released on his own reconnaissance or his own recognizance?

93

(a) What is the difference between a man who is amiable and one who is amicable?

(b) Between one who is complaisant and one who is complacent?

(c) One who is envious and one whose actions are invidious?

(d) A machine which is mobile and one which is movable?

(e) A person who is provident and another who is prudent?

The above list of doublets is only partial. A fuller list can be found in Skeat's *Concise Etymological Dictionary*.

IX

Word Derivation: Greek

OF THE many Greek words and roots that appear in English words, a knowledge of a few is of general usefulness.

In the following exercises learn the meaning of each English word and notice how much of the meaning of the original Greek word remains.

94

    (a) *Aster*, a star: *asterisk, astrology, disaster.*
        Why is a disaster so called?
    (b) *Bios*, life: *amphibious, biography, biology.*
    (c) *Gamos*, marriage: *bigamy, monogamy, polygamy.*
    (d) *Genos*, race: *genesis, geneology, endogen.*
    (e) *Kratus*, strong: *autocracy, aristocracy, democrat, plutocrat.*

95

    (a) *Grapho*, write: *autograph, lithograph, telegram, anagram, epigram, diagram.*
    (b) *Derma*, skin: *epidermis, pachyderm.* Does a pachyderm have an epidermis? Is *pachyderm*, when applied to human beings, a term of flattery?
    (c) *Theos*, a god: *apotheosis, atheism, pantheism, theocracy. theology.*

(d) *Krypto*, hide: *crypt, apocrypha, cryptogram, cryptogamia.*

(e) *Logos*, a saying: *analogue, catalogue, decalogue, dialogue, logic, monologue, prologue, astrology, theology, zoology.*

96 With the help of a large dictionary, trace the meanings of the Greek words that help to form the following sets of English words; determine how much of the original Greek meaning is left in the English word:

(a) *Monarch, monad, monochord, monoplane, monogram.*

(b) *Barometer, ammeter, geometer.*

(c) *Anonymous, metonymy, onomatopoeia, patronymic, pseudonym, synonym.*

(d) *Antipathy, sympathy, apathy.*

(e) *Petrify, petroleum.*

(f) *Anachronism, chronicle, chronology, chronometer, isochronous, synchronous.*

(g) *Sophomore, philosopher, sophisticated.*

(h) *Philanthropy, Philadelphia, Anglophile, philosophy.*

(i) *Hydrophobia, Anglophobia, claustrophobia.*

X

Fun With The Dictionary And Other Wordbooks

READING the dictionary is fun, particularly if you use a large unabridged dictionary such as Webster's *New International Dictionary* or Funk and Wagnall's *New Standard Dictionary*. If you will look up a common word, *grand* for instance, in one of these wonderful volumes, you will find that the dictionary gives within a small space the following facts about the word and aids in understanding it:

1. the accepted spelling
2. the part of speech
3. the accent
4. the syllabification (when the word has two or more syllables)
5. the pronunciation
6. the definition or definitions
7. phrases or sentences, often drawn from the prose and poetry of standard English writers, illustrating the proper uses of the word
8. occasional illustrations in picture form
9. the present standing of the word in the language, whether slang, or rare, or obsolete, or poetic, etc.

10. the use and meaning of the word in special phrases and combinations (for instance *grandfather*) and in idiomatic constructions
11. the most common synonyms, and a discussion of their differences in meaning and use
12. the most common antonyms
13. the derivation: that is, the parent word from which the word has originally stemmed; and other forms that the word has assumed on its way into English and after it had become a part of our language
14. cognates of the word: that is, other words that have stemmed from the same root

There is much that is amusing in a large dictionary. If you will look up *precocious*, you will find that it literally means "pre-cooked" or "pre-ripened." A precocious child, one who is far ahead of himself mentally, is like a fruit or a vegetable that has ripened too early. Another interesting word is *egregious*. Literally it means "from out the flock"; it suggests that one has been chosen from the rest of the flock because of some distinguishing characteristic. The word was once used in a complimentary sense, but it is now used chiefly in such expressions as "an egregious fool" or "an egregious dunce," implying that the distinguishing characteristic for which the egregious person has been "chosen out of the flock" is not an admirable one.

The verb *to shilly-shally*, meaning to vacillate in the making of a decision, is interesting too, for it was originally "Shill I, shall I," "shill" being another form of "shall." It is obvious how the word came to have its present meaning. Again, the word *dandelion*, the dictionary tells us, comes from the French *dent de lion*, meaning "tooth of a lion." The name was suggested by the ragged leaves of the plant.

Nonce, in the expression "for the nonce" (meaning "for the occasion only"), was originally *for than anes* (*for the once*). The final *n* of *than* moved forward to become a part of *anes*. *Nanes* grew slowly into modern *nonce*.

A similar shift of the final consonant of the preceding word to make the initial consonant of a following word occurred in the following:

> *a newt* was originally *an ewt*
> *a nickname* was once *an eke-name*
> *mine uncle* was originally *my nuncle;* **hence our**
> modern word *uncle*
> *an adder* was once *a nadder*

It must be confessed that the standard dictionaries, even in unabridged form, are not always satisfactory in their explanations of the derivation of a word, especially from the point of view of a novice. The essential information, to be sure, is presented in compact form, but often a considerable degree of imagination is necessary if one is to see the relationship between the meaning of the parent word and its modern descendant, and the intervening steps in the history of a word are sometimes clear only to one who has had considerable practice in tracing the history of words. Webster's *New International Dictionary* is, from this point of view, superior to the Funk and Wagnall's *New Standard Dictionary*. One or the other of these volumes is always obtainable in any sizeable school library or public library.

The student should understand the most frequently used abbreviations employed by the editors of each of these dictionaries. Let us look up in the *New Standard Dictionary*, by way of practice, the two words *alimony* and *compunction* and see how the etymological information is presented. In both dictionaries this information is given within square brackets.

[< L. *alimonia*, < *alo*, nourish.]

Which, being interpreted, means that *alimony* is directly derived from the Latin *alimonia*, which in turn comes from *alo*, meaning "to nourish." The symbol < means "is derived from."

The facts about the derivation of *compunction* are presented thus:

[< L.L. *compunctio* (n–), < L. *compunctus*, *pp.* of *compungo*, sting, < *com*– (<*cum*) intens. + *pungo*, sting.]

This means that the modern English *compunction* is derived from the Late Latin *compunctio* (other forms of which add -*n*), which in turn is derived from the Latin *compunctus*, the past participal of *compungo*, meaning *sting*, which comes from *com* (derived from *cum*) used intensively (that is, to add emphasis) plus *pungo*, meaning "sting."

Webster's *New International Dictionary* uses almost the same set of symbols, but it employs "fr." in the sense of "is derived from" in the place of Funk and Wagnall's <. The derivation of *acorn* is recorded as follows:

[M.E. *akern*, fr. AS. *æcern*.]

These symbols mean that *acorn* has come from the Middle English *akern*, which in turn came from the Anglo-Saxon *aecern*.

The modern *biography* is derived from the Greek *biographia*, a word from the Greek *bios*, meaning "life," and *graphein*, "to write." Webster records this information thus:

[Gr. *biographia*, fr. *bios*, life + *graphein*, to write]

Sometimes a good deal of space is needed to record all essential etymological information. *Remorse* in its present form and sense is derived from the Middle English *remors*, which comes direct from the Old

French *remors* (*remords* in French), derived from
Late Latin *remorsus*, which came from the Latin
remordere, *remorsum* (meaning "to bite again or back"
and "to torment") derived from the Latin *re-* (meaning
just what *re-* does in modern English, namely "again";
e. g. "reopen") combined with Latin *mordere*, meaning "to bite." There is a similarity of derivation between *remorse* and *morsel*; the two words are cognates.
All this information Webster presents in this brief
manner:

> [M.E. *remors*, fr. OF. *remors* (F. *remords*),
> fr. LL. *remorsus*, fr. L. *remordere*, *remorsum*,
> to bite again or back, to torment, fr. *re-re-* +
> *mordere*, to bite. See MORSEL.]

97 As practice, look up in the dictionary the word
sarcophagus. Notice its meaning and its pronunciation
and then study the etymological symbols. "Gr." means
"Greek"; the abbreviation "cf." means "compare," or
"look up." You will find under *sarcophagus* that Webster refers you to *sarcasm* and *sarcoma*. Look up these
words too, and after noticing their meanings and pronunciation observe that the element "sar-", which
forms a part of all three of the words, has the same
meaning and conveys a part of the idea expressed by
each word.

98 The following words have been selected both
for their particular etymological interest and for the

ease with which their origins may be understood from the information given in Webster's *New International Dictionary* and often in other sizable dictionaries. When you study each word, be sure to notice the pronunciation and the meaning, even if you think you already know them; sometimes you will be astonished at what you learn:

accumulate	defalcate	pedagogue	tantalize*
aftermath	delirium	trivial	prevaricate
aggravate	enthrall*	procrastinate	
alimony	expedite	recalcitrant	
ambiguous	incise	remorse	
anecdote	instill	sarcophagus	
blunderbuss	libertine	stigma	
bowdlerize	milliner	stoic	
boycott	nasturtium	succinct*	
compunction	parasite	superfluous	
curfew	pecuniary	symposium	

The process by which many of our English words have come to have their present-day meanings will be obscure to the beginner if he relies only on the dictionary. Fortunately, there are many other books designed to help him understand the history of words and the manner in which their meanings have become attached to them. One of the best of such books for a

* When studying *enthrall*, be sure to look up *thrall* also.
  Note the definitions of *succinct*.
  The meaning of *tantalize* can be understood fully only if you look up *Tantalus*.

student just beginning to investigate the origin of words is called *Picturesque Word Origins*, the author of which is unnamed, but published by G. and C. Merriam Company of Springfield, Massachusetts. As its title suggests, this book is copiously illustrated.

Other interesting and useful books are these; the books marked with asterisks are considered to be of particular value to anyone just beginning to study the origins of words:

Emerson, O. F., *History of the English Language*
* Fowler, H. W. and F. G., *The King's English*,
  1934, pp. 18–68
* Greenough and Kittredge, *Words and Their Ways
  in English Speech*
Jespersen, O., *The Growth and Structure of the
  English Language*
* Kent, R. G., *Language and Philology*, 1932, pp.
  26–38 and 58–76
* McKnight, G. H., *English Words and Their
  Background*
Mencken, H. L., *The American Language*
Skeat, W. W., *Etymological Dictionary*
* Skeat, W. W., *A Concise Etymological Dictionary*
* Smith, L. P., *Words and Idioms*
* Weekley, E., *The Romance of Words*
* Weckley, E., *Etymological Dictionary of Modern
  English*
* Weekley, E., *The Romance of Names*
* Weekley, E., *Adjectives — and Other Words*
* Weekley, E., *A Concise Etymological Dictionary
  of Modern English*

* Weekley, E., *Words Ancient and Modern*
* Weekley, E., *More Words Ancient and Modern*
* Weekley, E., *Something About Words*
  Wyld, H. C., *A Universal Dictionary of the English Language*

These are only a few of the many interesting books written about English words. Investigate the shelves of your public library and see what else you can find on the same subject.

99 Making use of some of the books mentioned above or of any other books that you can find, look up the meanings of the following words, remembering in each case to learn the pronunciation and the meaning of the word also·

(a) abet, suspicious, bugle, eliminate, preposterous
(b) abeyance, assassin, escape, pariah, vandal
(c) abominate, bedlam, congregation, fool, investigate
(d) bombastic, chivalry, pavilion, sacrifice, steward
(e) budget, dunce, easel, harangue, impediment
(f) inaugurate, libel, opportune, precipitate, ruminate

100 Using any books of reference to which you have access, try to answer the following questions:

(a) What does *abject* have to do with the idea of throwing? In what sense is an abject man "thrown away"?

(b) What connection is there between *agony* and ancient Greek athletic contests?

(c) How is *anatomy* connected with the idea of cutting?

(d) What does *deliberate* have to do with a pair of scales?

(e) How is *journey* connected with the idea of "day"?

(f) What relationship is there between a panic and an ancient Greek god?

(g) How are *record* and the human heart related in meaning?

(h) What does a taxicab have to do with a goat?

(i) What does the adjective *subtle* have in common with a weaver's loom?

101 What connection is there between

(a) *abundance* and a wave
(b) *accost* and a rib
(c) *chapel* and a cloak
(d) *companion* and bread
(e) *fee* and a cow
(f) *astonish* and thunder
(g) *bonfire* and bones
(h) *canopy* and gnats
(i) *torrid* and a torrent
(j) an *ambulance* and walking
(k) *marmalade* and apples
(l) *pencils* and little tails
(m) *rehearsals* and plows
(n) a *salary* and salt
(o) a *supercilious* person and eyebrows

XI

Slang and Idiom

SINCE a study of slang is of little benefit to anyone who wishes to enlarge his stock of standard words, it would not be to the purpose for this book to devote much space to it. It is well, however, to mention in passing that the continuous creation of slang terms is part of the natural process of language-making, that it is often forceful and picturesque, and that slang expressions frequently rise to be acceptable colloquialisms and even parts of our formal vocabulary. But as a general rule, slang lacks dignity and is often cheap and vulgar. No doubt it has its appropriate occasions, and it is a fascinating subject of study; but as McKnight points out, "Slang is considerably below the level of common speech," and its use "checks the acquisition of a command over recognized modes of expression." This book recognizes that educated people habitually speak and write in two different ways, as the occasion demands; one of their vocabularies is highly colloquial, and the other is formal or "literary." Since it is the latter kind of vocabulary with which this book is concerned, it is sufficient to refer anyone who is interested in slang to the following:

McKnight, G. H., *English Words and Their Background*, Chapter IV

TWELVE WAYS TO BUILD A VOCABULARY

Greenough and Kittredge, *Words and Their Ways in English Speech*, Chapter VI

Partridge's *A Dictionary of English Slang and Unconventional English*

Mencken, H. L., *The American Language*

Farmer and Henley's *Dictionary of Slang and Colloquial English*

Though a study of slang is not to the purpose in such a book as this, idiom is much a matter of its concern, for as Logan Pearsall Smith* points out, idiom is "the life and spirit of language." The difference between slang and idiom is not great, for almost all idiom was once slang that has risen to become a part of the conventional English vocabulary.

"Idiom," as used in this book, means those phrases peculiar to the English language which ignore the laws of grammar or the laws of logic but which are nevertheless "good English." Considered literally, word for word, idioms often do not make good sense, but the meaning of the phrase as a whole is perfectly clear. Such idioms as "on hand," "for good and all," "to put up with," and "to take to one's heels" are logical nonsense, yet we use them every day and never hesitate over their meaning. English idioms translated word for word into another language are usually meaningless and at best are awkward and unnatural. *Faire tête*

---

* This chapter is indebted to a delightful and useful book, *Words and Idioms*, by Logan Pearsall Smith; Houghton Mifflin and Company, 1925.

contre, for example, is an insane hodgepodge to the ear of a Frenchman, but literally translated into English, it is the common idiom *to make head against*.

A large number of English idioms are made from such common verbs as *fall, come, get, go, lay, look, set, stand, run, take, put, keep, hold, pull*, and *make* in various combinations with such prepositions (and prepositions used as adverbs) as *at, by, to, in, on, with, without, of, off, out, down, for, under, above, over, upon, against, behind*, and *along*. The verb *to come*, for example, combines to make such idioms as *to come at, to come by, to come to, to come in, to come on, to come of, to come off, to come out, to come down, to come for, to come under, to come over, to come upon, to come along, to come against*, and so on. Notice that some of these idioms have more than one meaning; e. g., *I can not come at the answer to this problem*, and *The elephant came at the hunter*.

Common verbs like those listed in the preceding paragraph combine also with adjectives, adverbs, and nouns to form familiar idioms: *to make good, to run low, to make friends*. A profuse source of idioms is the human body in its various parts: *to keep one's head, to nose out, to see eye to eye with, to turn a deaf ear, to set one's heart on, to change hands, to stand on one's own legs, to put one's best foot forward*, and hundreds of others.

The great writers of English, with a few notable exceptions, have used idiom freely. Walter Savage Landor states that "every good writer has much idiom; it is the life and spirit of language." Shakespeare, Swift, Addison, Sterne, Dryden, and Lamb, to name but a few, abound in the use of idiom. Robert Louis Stevenson uses so much idiom that the practice becomes almost an affectation with him. Idiom gives energy and color to language which otherwise might become dull and insipid. It is a part of our language that we could ill do without.

102 Try to think of idiomatic expressions containing the word *head* and meaning the following:

    (a) to become excited and bewildered
    (b) to be intelligent
    (c) to be conceited
    (d) to conceive an idea
    (e) to talk endlessly
    (f) to progress
    (g) beyond one's intelligence

103 What idioms containing the word *face* mean the following?

    (a) to be impudent enough to
    (b) to become opposed to
    (c) to grimace
    (d) to appear courageous

(e) to make one's appearance
(f) to accuse someone with
(g) to be hypocritical

104 Think of all the idioms that you can which contain the following words; use each idiomatic expression in a sentence and explain the meaning of the idiom:

(a) eye(s)
(b) nose
(c) ear (s)
(d) mouth
(e) teeth

105 Find idiomatic phrases containing the following words. What is the meaning of each of the idioms that you have formed?

(a) tongue
(b) blood
(c) heart
(d) hand
(e) foot

106 What is the meaning of each of the following idiomatic phrases? (Notice that all of them are drawn from the life of the sea.)

(a) to drop the pilot
(b) to lay an anchor to windward

(c) to nail one's flag to the mast
(d) to show one's colors
(e) to stem the tide
(f) all at sea
(g) not a shot in the locker
(h) to take in a reef

107 What do the following idioms mean? Use each in a sentence. (From what do they all seem to come?)

(a) to take the bit in one's teeth
(b) to give a leg up
(c) at the end of one's tether
(d) well in hand
(e) to look a gift-horse in the mouth
(f) to come a cropper
(g) to give one his head

108 What do the following idioms, drawn from the life of mills and shops, mean when used in ordinary English speech and writing?

(a) to put through the mill
(b) all is grist that comes to the mill
(c) to have too many irons in the fire
(d) in full blast
(e) to have an axe to grind
(f) not to put too fine a point on it
(g) the thin end of the wedge
(h) a chip off the old block
(i) to stick to one's last

109   The following idioms are Biblical in origin. Use each in a sentence and explain what the idiom means:

  (a) all things to all men
  (b) new wine in old bottles
  (c) weighed in the balance
  (d) whited sepulchres
  (e) a labor of love
  (f) the apple of the eye
  (g) the fleshpots of Egypt
  (h) to see eye to eye with
  (i) to strain at a gnat
  (j) to be built upon sand

110   Shakespeare's plays provide us with many idiomatic expressions. What is the meaning of each of the following:

  (a) to give the Devil his due
  (b) to wear one's heart on one's sleeve
  (c) to do yeoman service
  (d) a foregone conclusion
  (e) an itching palm
  (f) the primrose path
  (g) to the manner born
  (h) sermons in stones
  (i) caviar to the general

111   What is the meaning of each of the following idioms?

  (a) to make after, away with, for, off, off with,
       out, over, up, up to

(b) to give away, back, forth, in, in to, out, over, up; given to

(c) to hang about, back, on, over, out, upon

(d) to put about, aside, away, back, by, down, forth, forward, in, off, on, out, up, upon, to

(e) to go about, after, against, ahead, astray, back, before, by, down, forth, off, on, out, over, through, under, up, with

(f) to take after, aside, down, for, off, on, to, in, up

N. B. Notice that some of the idioms listed above have more than one meaning.

112   Get a copy of Stevenson's *Kidnapped* or of one of his short stories, such as *The Sire de Malétroit's Door*, and make a list of the idioms which he uses in the first ten pages of each. Are any of the idioms unfamiliar in American usage? Is the meaning of the unfamiliar idiom nevertheless clear to you?

113   In your reading, keep your eyes open for idioms that are unfamiliar to you. Learn what they mean, and make them a part of your vocabulary.

(a) Open a copy of one of Shakespeare's plays at random and make a list of the idioms to be found on any two of his pages.

(b) Do the same with a novel by Scott.

(c) Do the same with the whole of Milton's *Lycidas,* or *L'Allegro,* or *Il Penseroso.*

(d) Investigate one of the novels of Thomas
Hardy in the same way; remember that he is
writing about a small and heterogeneous section of England, and try to find idioms used
by the characters in their conversation that
are unfamiliar to you. Such idioms are probably provincialisms.

(e) Get hold of a volume of Gibbon's *Decline
and Fall of the Roman Empire* and analyze
five or six pages to see how many idioms the
writer seems to use in his ordinary flow of
writing. What conclusion can you draw
about his English prose style?

(f) Talk with someone who has a good knowledge of French and ask him about the fre-
quency of idiom in that language. Ask him
to translate some common French idioms into
literal English, and notice how strange most
of them sound.

XII

Prefixes

A PREFIX is a syllable or word-element used as the first part of a word and to some degree modifying its meaning. *Antenatal* means "before birth," and *postnatal* means "after birth," the difference of meaning, obviously, being expressed by the prefixes *ante-* and *post-*. A telescope is an instrument used for seeing afar, and a microscope is one designed for seeing small objects. The entire difference of meaning between the two words is conveyed by the prefixes, for *tele* is the Greek word for "far," and *mikros* is the Greek for "small."

The study of prefixes is one of some difficulty and should not be attempted until some mastery of the previous parts of this book has been obtained. Difficulty arises especially from the fact that the meaning of many English prefixes has been so thoroughly absorbed into the meaning of the entire word of which it is a part that the force of the prefix is not apparent except to advanced students. In the following pages, however, a selection has been made of the most common and useful prefixes. A knowledge of the meanings of these word elements is frequently of help in getting at the meaning of an unfamiliar word.

114 *A-* in the following words means "not": *amoral, achromatic, adamant, agamic, agnostic, amaranth, amnesty, anaemic, anesthetic, anarchy, anecdote, anodyne, anomalous, anonymous, apathy, aseptic, asexual, asphyxia, astigmatic.* With the help of a good dictionary learn the meanings of these words and notice how the negative idea is supplied by the prefix.

115 *Ambi-, Amphi-,* and *Amb-* mean " on both sides," "around." How do they contribute to the meanings of these words: *ambassador, amputate, ambidextrous, amphitheatre, ambiguous, ambient, amphibious,* and *amphora?*

116 *Antediluvian, antedate, antepenultimate,* and *ancestor* all contain the idea of "before"; what is the meaning of each word?

117 *Antarctic, anticlimax, antidote, antimacassar, antinomian, antipathy, antiphon, antipodes, antiseptic, antithesis, antitoxin,* and *antitype* contain the idea of "against, opposite to." What is the meaning of each word?

118 *Auto-* means "self." What similarity is there between an *automobile,* an *automaton,* an *autopsy,* an *autobiography,* an *autocrat,* an *autograph,* and *autonomy?*

119 Explain how the idea of "two" enters into the following words: *bicycle, biceps, bicuspid, biennial, bifoliate, bifurcate, bigamy, bilateral, bilingual, bimetallism, binocular, biped, bireme, bisect, bivalve.*

120 *Benediction, benefaction, benefice, beneficent, beneficiary,* and *benevolent* all contain the idea of "well." What is the meaning of each word?

121 Know the meanings of the words in each of the following groups:

(a) *Circumambient, circumflex, circumfluent, circumjacent, circumnavigate, circumspect, circumvallation, circumvent.*
(b) *Coagulate, corrode, coaxial, cognate, collocutor, colloquy, concatenation, concomitant, confluent, congener, conjunction, consanguinity.* What idea is common to all these words?
(c) *Contrapuntal, contradict, contravene.*
(d) *Decalcify, desecrate, desiccate, devious.* What is the common meaning of *de-*?

122 What is the force of the prefix in the words of each of the following groups? What is the meaning of each word?

(a) *Demigod, demilune, demimonde*

(b) *Dilemma, disyllable, digraph, diploma, diphthong*

(c) *Duologue, duumvir, duplicity*

123

(a) If *Eu-* means "well," what meanings have the following words? *Eugenic, euphemism, euphony, eulogy, euphuism, eupeptic, eucalyptus?*

(b) *Homo-* means "same"; how does the meaning of "same" play a part in the meaning of these words: *homophone, homogeneous, homonym, homologous?*

(c) What idea is common both to *intercolumniation* and *interlocutor?*

(d) *Intra-* means "within"; what is the meaning of *intramural?*

(e) *Juxta-* means "next to"; what does *juxtapose* mean?

124 *Mal-* in the following words means "bad" or "badly"; explain the meaning of each word: *maladroit, malady, malapropos, malfeasance, malaria,* and *malison.*

125 Learn the meanings of the words in the groups that follow, and see how actively the prefix enters into the meaning of the word:

(a) *Misadventure, misnomer, miscreant, misprision, misanthrope, misalliance, misappropriate, misfeasance.*

(b) *Monochrome, monody, monogamy, monolith, monologue, monometallism, monopoly,
monotheism, monotone.*

(c) *Multifarious, multipartite, multiplicity.*

(d) *Nondescript, nonentity.*

(e) *Palimpsest, palindrome, palinode, palingenesis* (The prefix has the meaning of "again").

126

(a) If *Per-* means "through" or "by," what is the
meaning of *peradventure, perambulate, per-
colate, peregrinate, perennial, perfidy, per-
functory, permeate.*

(b) *Peri-* means "around"; what is the meaning
of *perihelion, perimeter, peripatetic, peri-
phery, periscope, peristyle.*

(c) If *Poly-* means "many," what is the meaning
of these words: *Polyandry, polychromatic,
polygamy, polyglot, polytheism, polysyllable?*

(d) In the following words, *Post-* has the meaning of "after"; what is the meaning of each
word? *Postdiluvian, postnatal, postprandial.*

(e) If *Pre-* and *Prae-* mean "before," determine
the meaning of each of the following words,
using a good dictionary to help you: *premonition, preprandial, precession, pre-empt,
praenomen, preposterous, prescient, presenti-
ment, previous.*

127

(a) *Preter-* means "beyond." What are the meanings of *preterhuman, preternatural, preter-
mit?*

(b) If *Retro-* means "backwards" or "behind," what is the meaning of *retrograde, retrogress, retrochoir, retrospect?*

(c) What is the meaning of *Semi-* in *semitone, semi-official, semichorus?*

(d) *Sub-* means "under," "beneath," and "below." Find the meanings of *subaqueous, subaudition, subcutaneous, subjacent, sublunary, subsidy,* and *substratum.*

(e) *Super-* means "above" or "over." What are the meanings of *superciliary, superfluous, supermundane, supernumerary, supersede?*

128

The prefix (*Sym-, Syl-,* and *Syn-*) common to the following words means "with" or "together with." Be sure you know the meaning of each word and keep in mind the force of the prefix. *Sympathy, symmetry, symphony, symposium, syllogism, syntax, synagogue, synchronous, syncopate, syndicate, synod, synonym, synopsis.*

129

(a) *Tele-* means "afar." What meaning has *telegony, telepathy, telegraph, telephone, telescope?* What is the difference between a telescope and a microscope, and how does the prefix of each of these words determine the meaning?

(b) *Tra-*, *Tran-*, and *Trans-* mean "across" in the words of the following list. What is the meaning of *trajectory*, *transatlantic*, *transept*, *transfuse*, *transfigure*, *transitory*, *transliterate*, *translucent*, *transmigration*, *transubstantiate?*

(c) What meaning have the following words in common? *Triceps*, *trigonometry*, *triangle*, *trichromatic*.

(d) What meaning is common to the prefixes of all the following words: *univocal*, *unilateral*, *unicameral*, *unicorn*, *uniform*, *univalve*, *universal?*

130 This is an advanced exercise for those who wish to pursue the subject of prefixes. In the words that follow, the meaning of the prefixes is not so obvious as in the words included in the previous exercises. The student will need to refer constantly to a large dictionary.

(a) How much of the meaning of the prefix is apparent in the meaning of these words: *ablution*, *abnegate*, *aboriginal*, *abrogate*, *abstemious*, *abscond?*

(b) Study the meaning of the following words and observe the force of the prefix: *acclivity*, *accolade*, *accretion*, *adumbrate*, *adventitious*, *afflatus*, *agglomerate*, *agglutinate*, *agnate*, *alluvium*, *amerce*.

(c) Do the same with *anagram, anabaptist, anachronism, analogue, analysis, anapest, anathema,* and *aneurism.* Has the force of the prefix been forgotten in the meaning of the English words?

131 This exercise is for advanced readers. Use a good dictionary to determine the meanings of the prefixes and notice whether the prefix has any force in each of the English words:

(a) *Archbishop, archangel, architect, archetype.*

(b) *Catechism, catholic, catacomb, cataclysm, catalepsy, catalogue, catapult, cataract, catarrh, catastrophe, category.*

(c) *Diabetes, diagnosis, diagram, diaphanous, diaphragm, diathesis, diorama, diatribe.*

(d) *Epoch, ephemeral, epicene, epicycle, epidemic, epidermis, epigram, epilepsy, epilogue, epithet, epitome, eponymous.*

(e) *Exacerbate, excogitate, excoriate, excrescent, exculpate, execrate, exfoliate, exonerate, exorcize, exordium, exude.*

(f) *Heteroclite, heterodox, heterogeneous.*

(g) *Hyperbole, hyperborean, hypertrophy, hypercritical.*

(h) *Hypocaust, hypochondria, hypodermic, hypothesis.*

(i) *Imbrue, impeccable.*

(j) *Metabolism, metamorphosis, metaphor, metempsychosis, metonymy.*

(k) *Obdurate, obese, obfuscate, obloquy, obnoxious, obstreperous, obviate, occult, opprobrium.*

(l) *Pantomime, panacea, pancreas, pandemonium, panoply, panorama, pantograph.*

132   Also for advanced readers. Do the same with the following words as with those in Section 131:

(a) *Parody, paraclete, paradigm, paradox.*

(b) *Proboscis, proclivity, procrastinate, profligate, progenitor, prognostic, program, prolocutor, prolix.*

(c) *Protagonist, protoplasm, prototype.*

(d) *Recriminate, relegate, reagent, recalcitrant, recension, recrudescence, redintegrate, redundant, refrangible, refulgent, regenerate, regurgitate, reiterate, rejuvenate, renaissance, renegade, replete, reprobate, retaliate.*

(e) *Secede, segregate.*

(f) *Subterfuge.*

HOW MANY DO YOU KNOW?

How Many Do You Know?

THE ten Vocabulary Tests which follow are not calculated to be of equal difficulty and should perhaps be regarded less as tests than as devices for arousing curiosity and as instruments for building vocabulary. Keys to the tests will be found following Test Number 10.

Each test contains twenty-five italicized words incorporated in phrases or sentences. After each phrase or sentence are five words, one of which is to be chosen as being closest in meaning to the preceding italicized word. Indicate the word which you have chosen by underlining it. For example:

The *large* book: old; flat; beautiful; big; red.

The word *big* should be underlined as being closest in meaning to *large*.

VOCABULARY TEST NO. 1.

1. Read with *avidity:* understanding; fear; eagerness; complaint; difficulty.
2. An *azure* shield: sky-blue; dented; battered; historic; mended.
3. A *blatant* note: coarse; soft; harmonious; commanding; inaudible.

4. A *bowdlerized* edition: expensive; first; expurgated; unprintable; advertised.

5. A *cognate* language: difficult; universal; ancient; kindred; musical.

6. A reward *commensurate* with service: earned; deserved; proportionate; determined; promised.

7. We *compensated* the lawyer: consoled; engaged; paid; quizzed; advised.

8. His essay was *discursive:* brief; enlightening; rambling; harsh; severely critical.

9. A *disinterested* person: uninformed; impartial; inattentive; uninteresting; unemotional.

10. A *diurnal* task: impossible; necessary; daily; occasional; urgent.

11. He *doffed* his armor: put-on; repaired; polished; removed; pledged.

12. *Evanescent* fashions: foolish; unvarying; universal; impermanent; fastidious.

13. An *infamous* person: wicked; obscure; unknown; noteworthy; fierce.

14. *Invaluable* documents: illegal; invalid; worthless; priceless; inadequate.

15. Exhausted by *lucubration:* long walks; lecturing; exposure; laborious study; intensive drill.

16. Influenced by his *machinations:* lies; desires; plots; fabulous tales; enemies.

17. A *mnemonic* device: self-adjusting; automatic; new; rust-proof; memory-assisting.

18. A *nondescript* appearance: unattractive; unclassifiable; ordinary; neat; favorable.

19. *Piceous* material: discarded; valuable; stony; inflammable; carefully selected.
20. He *recanted* the statement: repeated; denied; regretted; remembered; retracted.
21. The house was *razed:* rebuilt; elevated; rented; demolished; plundered.
22. The mob was *rampageous:* determined; easily influenced; large; boastful; disorderly.
23. *Sudoriferous* glands: tear; sleep-producing; mucous; hair-producing; sweat-producing.
24. A *sumptuous* house: luxurious; ornate; old-fashioned; artistic; substantial.
25. A *turgid* arm: swollen; strong; bent; wiry; useless.

VOCABULARY TEST NO. 2.

1. It caused an *abrasion:* infection; wearing away; rebellion; reunion; revision.
2. *Actuated* by greed: driven; disgusted; repelled; defeated; denounced.
3. He is a *bacchanal:* Baptist; biologist; critic; rustic; reveler.
4. Expressions of great *compunction:* relief; earnestness; despair; praise; remorse.
5. A *corvine* cry: crow-like; blood-curdling; loud; inaudible; startled.
6. *Dapper* yachts: sailing; steam; trim; strong; anchored.
7. How have they *demeaned* themselves? debased; lowered; conducted; elevated; deceived.
8. *Execrable* verse: blank; serious; excellent; profound; wretched.
9. We cannot *forego* this: enjoy; profit by; give up; remember; anticipate.

10. He was too old to *gambol:* wager; jump about; speculate; play an instrument.

11. The *halcyon* days: peaceful; historic; ancient; memorable; disquieting.

12. *Immaculate* linen: homespun; threadbare; spotless; unwashed; preshrunk.

13. An unworthy *immolation:* suggestion; attempt; imitation; sacrifice; conclusion.

14. We sat in the *kirk:* church; bow; park; jail; gallery.

15. The flesh was *lacerated:* stimulated; torn; protected; examined; decayed.

16. A *Laconic* reply: sarcastic; impudent; concise; evasive; lengthy.

17. A *malodorous* plant: twisted; ill-smelling; poisonous; deadly; nutritious..

18. The witness was *maligned:* slandered; sworn-in; cross-examined; called; released.

19. *Necessitous* peasants: insistent; noisy; necessary; underfed; poverty-stricken.

20. The soldier was *obese:* obedient; stubborn; obeyed; very fat; unaccounted for.

21. A *palpable* error: excusable; obvious; unpardonable; disastrous; frequent.

22. A *ruthless* ruler: cruel; unloved; childless; democratic; ignorant.

23. A *sable* cloak: light; formal; threadbare; black; unbecoming.

24. The boy was *taciturn:* indifferent; habitually silent; discreet; very honest; extremely devout.

25. A *vacuous* face: intelligent; stupid; aristocratic; fascinating; flushed.

VOCABULARY TEST NO. 3.

1. Done with *alacrity:* unconcern; desperation; indecision; hope; briskness.
2. *Baleful* influence: helpful; destructive; inspiring; widespread; benevolent.
3. They were *constrained* to surrender: forced; advised; forbidden; asked; persuaded.
4. A *dearth* of material: abundance; division; diversity; confusion; insufficiency.
5. Such thoughts *debilitate* the mind: strengthen; stimulate; engross; weaken; fill.
6. This money has been *earmarke*d: set-aside; confiscated; counterfeited; protected; deposited.
7. A *feckless* piece of work: unusual; inimitable; faultless; worthless; priceless.
8. A *garrulous* person: easily deceived; friendly; trustworthy; talkative; energetic.
9. He is a *hedonist:* pagan; dog-fancier; fire-worshipper; pleasure-seeker; harpist.
10. An *immutable* law: unalterable; variable; uniform; disregarded; unjust.
11. We saw the *lama:* valley; venomous snake; crag; dromedary; high priest.
12. A *medicable* disease: malignant; fatal; curable; infectious; hereditary.
13. He is a *niggard:* half-breed; miser; octoroon; sailor; wizard.
14. An *obsolete* word: disused; slang; provincial; misused; inappropriate.
15. He was guilty of *peculation:* desertion; arson; murder; theft; lying.

16. The *quondam* king: enraged; former; peace-loving; exiled; gracious.
17. A *rubicund* face: oval; fat; ruddy; aristocratic; handsome.
18. *Rugose* skin: smooth; sunburned; oily; wrinkled; healthy.
19. *Salubrious* climate: damp; variable; insufferable; weakening; wholesome.
20. A *sardonic* expression: encouraging; sickly; sarcastic; confident; calm.
21. A *tenacious* memory: inaccurate; short; uncertain; retentive; vivid.
22. *Tepid* waters: foul; clear; hot; boiling; lukewarm.
23. An *unctuous* substance: hard; pliable; oily; gritty; poisonous.
24. A *veracious* historian: prejudiced; inaccurate; stimulating; truthful; careful.
25. A *wily* merchant: successful; wealthy; smart; crafty; independent.

VOCABULARY TEST NO. 4.

1. The boy was *amenable:* obstinate; manageable; intelligent; popular; curable.
2. A *banal* remark: wise; bright; audible; commonplace; humorous.
3. *Brumal* weather: balmy; winterlike; damp; penetrating; depressing.
4. We *consummated* the plan: considered; formed; worked-on; conceived-of; finished.
5. He *contravened* the law: voted-for; respected; violated; observed; supported.

6. We *decried* the play: praised; called-attention-to; condemned; advertised; reviewed.

7. An *edible* fruit: rare; luscious; eatable; ripe; cultivated.

8. A *ferine* cry: blood-curdling; catlike; wild; mournful; piercing.

9. The story was not *germane:* foreign; unknown; believable; fictitious; relevant.

10. The *hiatus* was of short duration: fever; friendship; insurrection; visit; interval.

11. *Impeccable* attire: inappropriate; faultless; customary; formal; strange.

12. He was *lampooned:* satirized; praised; surrounded; caught; struck.

13. He was warned against *mendicants:* liars; robbers; quack doctors; beggars; socialists.

14. A *nocent* dose: disagreeable; healing; harmful; useless; narcotic.

15. *Ocular* proof: positive; visual; questionable; scientific; probable.

16. A *petulant* child: spoiled; sickly; lovable; robust; cross.

17. A *risible* mistake: pardonable; laughable; inexcusable; costly; fatal.

18. *Salutary* policies: intricate; beneficial; secret; domestic; extensive.

19. A *sanguinary* contest: bloody; uneven; beneficial; decisive; hard-fought.

20. A *signal* accomplishment: unexpected; sole; difficult; notable; doubtful.

21. His wife was a *termagant:* quarrelsome woman; child-beater; invalid; spendthrift; miserly wretch.

22. *Titanic* efforts: futile; superhuman; sinister; frequent; untimely.

23. An *untoward* occurrence: unexpected; unusual; helpful; unfortunate; discouraging.
24. His style was *verbose:* wearisome; clear; individual; artistic; wordy.
25. A *wistful* look: painful; joyful; stern; uncertain; longing.

VOCABULARY TEST NO. 5.

1. The quotation was *apposite:* contradictory; brief; pertinent; poetic; well known.
2. An *aquiline* nose: Roman; keen; hooked; flat; small.
3. Characterized by *bathos:* anticlimax; pity; emotion; adventure; grief.
4. A *callow* youth: insincere; immature; malicious; obstinate; unmanageable.
5. Exposed to *calumny:* hatred; dishonesty; slander; praise; danger.
6. The city was *despoiled:* plundered; rebuilt; attacked; conquered; besieged.
7. He read in a *desultory* manner: determined; aimless; futile; mechanical; profitable.
8. *Enervating* climate: enfeebling; invigorating; humid; healthful; variable.
9. The plan was *frustrated:* completed; made clear; approved; voted upon; defeated.
10. Accomplished without *guile:* assistance; exhaustion; consent; treachery; interference.
11. *Ineffable* joys: supreme; deserved; unbearable; unforgettable; indescribable.
12. An *inexorable* ruler: unyielding; unjust; unloved; excellent; inexperienced.

13. A *limpid* stream: sluggish; shallow; winding; clear; peaceful.

14. A *mordant* comment: gloomy; sarcastic; pertinent; foolish; humorous.

15. *Opulent* citizens: hopeful; industrious; unfortunate; wealthy; indignant.

16. *Postprandial* speeches: political; soap-box; after-dinner; introductory; complimentary.

17. A *restive* horse: quiet; slow; impatient; retired; temperamental.

18. The law was *rescinded:* approved; repealed; amended; tested; violated.

19. They lived in *squalor:* poverty; isolation; confusion; contentment; filthiness.

20. *Sterile* land: unproductive; unused; fertile; unclaimed; cultivated.

21. *Sterling* qualities: undesirable; genuine; imaginary; undeveloped; unfortunate.

22. We *stipulated* payments in gold: refused; desired; specified; made; offered.

23. A *torpid* mind: diseased; active; keen; inquiring; dull.

24. *Vociferous* announcers: obstinate; ill-tempered; noisy; inaudible; ignorant.

25. He took his *wonted* position: abandoned; customary; desired; deserved; hard-won.

VOCABULARY TEST NO. 6.

1. An *anomalous* statement: unnoticed; irregular; obscure; misinterpreted; nameless.

2. An *apathetic* person: unconcerned; pitiful; disliked; appealing; skilled.

3. Money, the *bane* of his existence: support; ruin; chief aim; spark; goal.

4. The supply was *copious:* sufficient; inadequate; inexhaustible; abundant; intact.

5. A *corpulent* person: sociable; wealthy; fat; indiscreet; congenial.

6. The sentence was *deleted:* erased; revised; balanced; rewritten; shortened.

7. A *derelict* vessel: wrecked; chartered; disabled; stolen; abandoned.

8. An object of *derision:* approval; contempt; interest; value; attention.

9. The *effrontery* of the request: sincerity; importance; futility; impudence; purpose.

10. *Flaccid* flesh: firm; healthy; flabby; human; raw.

11. A *gnarled* stick: twisted; gnawed; seasoned; pointed; petrified.

12. *Hoary* fields: white; unplowed; fertile; barren; cultivated.

13. An *impecunious* cousin: thrifty; distant; poor; uncongenial; orphaned.

14. A *Laodicean* attitude: fierce; indifferent; warlike; cringing; defiant.

15. A *minatory* gesture: insignificant; fitting; awkward; brief; threatening.

16. In a *noisome* dungeon: dark; foul; damp; noisy; isolated.

17. An *odious* deed: odd; kind; hateful; brave; unexpected.

18. We *placated* the tribe: pacified; annihilated; organized; rescued; divided.

19. We *rifled* the box: restored; supported; picked-up; shot-through; robbed.

20. *Simian* features: similar; Jewish; irregular; clear-cut; apelike.
21. He is a *sluggard:* lazy-person; hard-hitter; foolish-investor; fortune-seeker; scout.
22. Cured of *somnambulism:* sleeplessness; sleepiness; sleepwalking; snoring; rheumatism.
23. A timely *tocsin:* arrival; injection; warning signal; friendly advice; medical attention.
24. An *urbane* citizen: loyal; very energetic; city-dwelling; respectable; courteous.
25. *Vesicated* skin: blistered; cut; tattooed; protected; exposed.

VOCABULARY TEST NO. 7.

1. He remained *adamant:* unyielding; incompetent; invaluable; unknown; unseen.
2. A mark of *affluence:* identity; wealth; heredity; self-denial; respect.
3. *Badgered* by creditors: ruined; assisted; worried; betrayed; bought.
4. A *congenital* weakness: confining; constitutional; incurable; painful; imaginary.
5. He sat on the *dais:* balcony; throne; railing; platform; step.
6. A *dauntless* soldier: cowardly; fearless; reckless; rash; useless.
7. The growth was *expedited:* hastened; retarded; excelled; expected; examined.
8. His suggestion was not *feasible:* supported; practicable; answerable; debatable; popular.
9. *Garish* decorations: suitable; expensive; showy; mural; soiled.

10. The *harbingers* of the storm: effects; announcers; causes; damages; victims.

11. He *immured* himself: immersed; initiated; scolded; vaccinated; imprisoned.

12. We listened to *jocund* strains: funereal; melancholy; lively; loud; soothing.

13. *Lacteal* fluid: transparent; inky; gaseous; milky; cold.

14. *Maculate* table linen: spotless; handmade; imported; unused; unclean.

15. A *nescient* officer: ignorant; obstinate; domineering; subordinate; cowardly.

16. The slave was *obsequious:* deceitful; reliable; unmanageable; disrespectful; fawning.

17. *Peccant* saints: complaining; holy; sinning; patron; avenging.

18. Meadows *riant* in the sunlight: fragrant; visible; green; smiling; growing.

19. *Sacrilegious* words: sacred; uncharitable; irreverent; very religious; unreligious.

20. *Salacious* stories: lively; interesting; misleading; lustful; incredible.

21. We avoided the *tatterdemalion:* detour; swamp; ragamuffin; rocky coast; sheriff.

22. *Ululant* hounds: hunting; howling; fierce; untamed; protecting.

23. *Venial* sins: premeditated; oft-repeated; excusable; unrepented; unpardonable.

24. He *waived* his right: claimed; relinquished; held; fought for; extended.

25. A worthy *wight:* deed; intention; person; resolution; enterprise.

VOCABULARY TEST NO. 8.

1. We visited the *apiary:* monastery; treasury; beehouse; apple orchard; ape cage.
2. Guilty of *apostasy:* indiscretion; theft; immorality; desertion; trickery.
3. A *Barmecide* feast: sumptuous; elaborate; imaginary; costly; barbarian.
4. A *crepitant* sound: rattling; soft; soothing; pleasing; suspicious.
5. A *cursory* examination: medical; trite; hasty; blasphemous; provoking
6. He spoke in *derogatory* terms: simple; confusing; injurious; exclamatory; technical.
7. He was *descried* by them: advised; described; denounced; discerned; painted.
8. A *desiccated* fish: cleaned; prehistoric; dried-up; maltreated; domesticated.
9. She gave an *eldritch* scream: pitiful; loud; feeble; angry; weird.
10. The *fiscal* year: current; previous; disappointing; financial; calendar.
11. A *flagitious* attack: unexpected; disastrous; wicked; overwhelming; bitter.
12. A just *guerdon:* account; judge; reward; verdict; penalty.
13. There's *husbandry* in heaven: contentment; thrift; marriage; brilliance; knowledge.
14. An *impious* deed: thoughtless; generous; unexpected; irreverent; unusual.
15. The poem was *lauded:* read; omitted; praised; copied; memorized.

16. A *momentous* decision: very important; quickly formed; short-lived; unanimous; wise.

17. A *nominal* fee: annual; fixed; relatively small; reasonable; unexpectedly exorbitant.

18. An *oleaginous* substance: ill-smelling; clayey; oily; bone-building; poisonous.

19. He is a *plagiarist:* writer of plays; literary thief; plague-bringer; pest; sculptor.

20. A *soporific* effect: beneficial; sleep-producing; harsh; feverish; body-building.

21. A *splenetic* reply: wise; carefully worded; forceful; ill-humored; gracious.

22. A *torose* back: broad; twisted; flabby; muscular; straight.

23. *Ursine* characteristics: bearlike; repulsive; inimitable; widely copied; clearly defined.

24. *Vitreous* rocks: hard; glass-like; pointed; dangerous; brittle.

25. A *wizened* old man: withered; exhausted; pathetic; wise; mistreated.

VOCABULARY TEST NO. 9.

1. We selected an *arbiter:* tool; manuscript; flower; judge; color.

2. Characterized by *asperity:* willingness; severity; simplicity; sweetness; tolerance.

3. The pain was *assuaged:* lessened; caused; developed; treated; intensified.

4. In a *bellicose* manner: abdominal; playful; opposite; serious; warlike.

5. A *candid* opinion: impartial; prejudiced; worthless; helpful; forced.

6. He is *capricious:* capable; changeable; constant; respected; industrious.

7. A *captious* companion: reliable; fascinating; curious; faultfinding; pleasant.

8. We watched the *caravel:* sailing vessel; company of travelers; fantastic dance; tropical snake; smoke.

9. A *devious* path: narrow; downhill; winding; inviting; direct.

10. A *diabolical* plan: constructive; acceptable; intricate; fiendish; unusual.

11. Its value was *enhanced:* appraised; reduced; raised; estimated; falsified.

12. A *gullible* race: proud; contemptible; readily ruled; warlike; easily deceived.

13. The act was *infamous:* unpopular; vile; unknown; obscure; voluntary.

14. A *lissom* lad: lonely; sad; awkward; stout; lithe.

15. *Mottled* wood: worm-eaten; decayed; petrified; spotted; carved.

16. A skillful *orthographist:* navigator; foot-doctor; explorer; economist; speller.

17. He had a reputation for *probity:* plain-speaking; fairness; dishonesty; integrity; stubbornness.

18. Subject to *reprehension:* relief; confusion; censure; responsibility; capture.

19. Unjustifiable *strictures:* misdemeanors; surrenders; refusals; censures; conclusions.

20. A *strident* voice: commanding; weak; sweet; powerful; shrill.

21. A *tortuous* trail: winding; narrow; dangerous; unexplored; picturesque.

22. *Tractable* children: selfish; easily managed; quarrelsome; easily found; suffering.
23. A *voracious* man: truthful; wise; dependable; gluttonous; sickly.
24. A *wry* face: pleasing; baffling; twisted; honest; deceptive.
25. A *xenial* custom: ancient; forgotten; commendable; hospitable; barbarous.

VOCABULARY TEST NO. 10.

1. An *astringent* effect: soothing; annoying; powerful; contracting; disastrous.
2. Destroyed by *attrition:* earthquake; friction; heat; command; parsimony.
3. The ranks of the *benedicks:* well-wishers; traitors; married men; prophets; boasters.
4. A man of *catholic* tastes: narrow; severe; liberal; intellectual; religious.
5. He is a *charlatan:* gentleman; officer; auditor; singer; impostor.
6. He resorted to *chicanery:* violence; trickery; logic; reasoning; intimidation.
7. A *chimerical* scheme: visionary; deceptive; contented; resourceful; rash.
8. A *choleric* man: diseased; bright; designing; hot-tempered; misunderstood.
9. *Diaphanous* cloth: homespun; coarse; heavy; transparent; expensive.
10. They commented on his *diffidence:* learning; contentment; dissimilarity; diction; shyness.

11. *Ephemeral* popularity: well-deserved; earned; enduring; short-lived; nation-wide.
12. *Innoxious* flames: consuming; spreading; harmless; colorless; smokeless.
13. An *inveterate* idler: unwilling; occasional; misunderstood; habitual; so-called.
14. The *littoral* regions: coastal; actual; imaginary; cultural; remote.
15. *Mundane* affairs: national; industrial; worldly; intellectual; secret.
16. An *otiose* boy: idle; shy; hateful; thin; bold.
17. Famous for his *prognostications:* witty words; manners; adventures; inventions; predictions.
18. He was never a *renegade:* doubter; philosopher; insurrectionist; volunteer; traitor.
19. A head *replete* with thoughts: filled; empty; crazed; enlarged; occupied.
20. *Stringent* requirements: severe; foolish; unfair; loose; illegal.
21. A *succinct* account: full; concise; inaccurate; colorful; exact.
22. A *transient* passion: intense; regrettable; short-lived; commendable; lasting.
23. *Truculent* tribes: unconquerable; wandering; defiant; ferocious; sociable.
24. A *vulnerable* fort: stoutly defended; ancient; unconquerable; weakening; assailable.
25. At the *zenith* of his career: beginning; end; middle; lowest point; highest point.

Keys to the Vocabulary Tests

KEY TO VOCABULARY TEST NO. 1.

1. *avidity* — eagerness
2. *azure* — sky-blue
3. *blatant* — coarse
4. *bowdlerized* — expurgated
5. *cognate* — kindred
6. *commensurate* — proportionate
7. *compensated* — paid
8. *discursive* — rambling
9. *disinterested* — impartial
10. *diurnal* — daily
11. *doffed* — removed
12. *evanescent* — impermanent
13. *infamous* — wicked
14. *invaluable* — priceless
15. *lucubration* — laborious study
16. *machinations* — plots
17. *mnemonic* — memory-assisting
18. *nondescript* — unclassifiable
19. *piceous* — inflammable
20. *recanted* — retracted
21. *razed* — demolished
22. *rampageous* — disorderly
23. *sudoriferous* — sweat-producing
24. *sumptuous* — luxurious
25. *turgid* — swollen

KEY TO VOCABULARY TEST NO. 2.

1. *abrasion* — wearing away
2. *actuated* — driven
3. *bacchanal* — reveler
4. *compunction* — remorse
5. *corvine* — crow-like
6. *dapper* — trim
7. *demeaned* — conducted
8. *execrable* — wretched
9. *forego* — give up
10. *gambol* — jump about
11. *halcyon* — peaceful
12. *immaculate* — spotless
13. *immolation* — sacrifice
14. *kirk* — church
15. *lacerated* — torn
16. *Laconic* — concise
17. *malodorous* — ill-smelling
18. *maligned* — slandered
19. *necessitous* — poverty-stricken
20. *obese* — very fat
21. *palpable* — obvious
22. *ruthless* — cruel
23. *sable* — black
24. *taciturn* — habitually silent
25. *vacuous* — stupid

KEY TO VOCABULARY TEST NO. 3.

1. *alacrity* — briskness
2. *baleful* — destructive
3. *constrained* — forced
4. *dearth* — insufficiency
5. *debilitate* — weaken
6. *earmarked* — set-aside
7. *feckless* — worthless
8. *garrulous* — talkative
9. *hedonist* — pleasure-seeker
10. *immutable* — unalterable
11. *lama* — high priest
12. *medicable* — curable
13. *niggard* — miser
14. *obsolete* — disused
15. *peculation* — theft
16. *quondam* — former
17. *rubicund* — ruddy
18. *rugose* — wrinkled
19. *salubrious* — wholesome
20. *sardonic* — sarcastic
21. *tenacious* — retentive
22. *tepid* — lukewarm
23. *unctuous* — oily
24. *veracious* — truthful
25. *wily* — crafty

KEY TO VOCABULARY TEST NO. 4.

1. *amenable* — manageable
2. *banal* — commonplace
3. *brumal* — winterlike
4. *consummated* — finished
5. *contravened* — violated
6. *decried* — condemned
7. *edible* — eatable
8. *ferine* — wild
9. *germane* — relevant
10. *hiatus* — interval
11. *impeccable* — faultless
12. *lampooned* — satirized
13. *mendicants* — beggars
14. *nocent* — harmful
15. *ocular* — visual
16. *petulant* — cross
17. *risible* — laughable
18. *salutary* — beneficial
19. *sanguinary* — bloody
20. *signal* — notable
21. *termagant* — quarrelsome woman
22. *Titanic* — superhuman
23. *untoward* — unfortunate
24. *verbose* — wordy
25. *wistful* — longing

KEYS TO THE VOCABULARY TESTS

KEY TO VOCABULARY TEST NO. 5.

1. *apposite* — pertinent
2. *aquiline* — hooked
3. *bathos* — anticlimax
4. *callow* — immature
5. *calumny* — slander
6. *despoiled* — plundered
7. *desultory* — aimless
8. *enervating* — enfeebling
9. *frustrated* — defeated
10. *guile* — treachery
11. *ineffable* — indescribable
12. *inexorable* — unyielding
13. *limpid* — clear
14. *mordant* — sarcastic
15. *opulent* — wealthy
16. *postprandial* — after-dinner
17. *restive* — impatient
18. *rescinded* — repealed
19. *squalor* — filthiness
20. *sterile* — unproductive
21. *sterling* — genuine
22. *stipulated* — specified
23. *torpid* — dull
24. *vociferous* — noisy
25. *wonted* — customary

KEY TO VOCABULARY TEST NO. 6.

1. *anomalous* — irregular
2. *apathetic* — unconcerned
3. *bane* — ruin
4. *copious* — abundant
5. *corpulent* — fat
6. *deleted* — erased
7. *derelict* — abandoned
8. *derision* — contempt
9. *effrontery* — impudence
10. *flaccid* — flabby
11. *gnarled* — twisted
12. *hoary* — white
13. *impecunious* — poor
14. *Laodicean* — indifferent
15. *minatory* — threatening
16. *noisome* — foul
17. *odious* — hateful
18. *placated* — pacified
19. *rifled* — robbed
20. *simian* — apelike
21. *sluggard* — lazy person
22. *somnambulism* — sleepwalking
23. *tocsin* — warning signal
24. *urbane* — courteous
25. *vesicated* — blistered

KEYS TO THE VOCABULARY TESTS

KEY TO VOCABULARY TEST NO. 7.

1. *adamant* — unyielding
2. *affluence* — wealth
3. *badgered* — worried
4. *congenital* — constitutional
5. *dais* — platform
6. *dauntless* — fearless
7. *expedited* — hastened
8. *feasible* — practicable
9. *garish* — showy
10. *harbingers* — announcers
11. *immured* — imprisoned
12. *jocund* — lively
13. *lacteal* — milky
14. *maculate* — unclean
15. *nescient* — ignorant
16. *obsequious* — fawning
17. *peccant* — sinning
18. *riant* — smiling
19. *sacrilegious* — irreverent
20. *salacious* — lustful
21. *tatterdemalion* — ragamuffin
22. *ululant* — howling
23. *venial* — excusable
24. *waived* — relinquished
25. *wight* — person

KEY TO VOCABULARY TEST NO. 8.

1. *apiary* — beehouse
2. *apostasy* — desertion
3. *Barmecide* — imaginary (Used only with **feast**)
4. *crepitant* — rattling
5. *cursory* — hasty
6. *derogatory* — injurious
7. *descried* — discerned
8. *desiccated* — dried-up
9. *eldritch* — weird
10. *fiscal* — financial
11. *flagitious* — wicked
12. *guerdon* — reward
13. *husbandry* — thrift
14. *impious* — irreverent
15. *lauded* — praised
16. *momentous* — very important
17. *nominal* — relatively small
18. *oleaginous* — oily
19. *plagiarist* — literary thief
20. *soporific* — sleep-producing
21. *splenetic* — ill-humored
22. *torose* — muscular
23. *ursine* — bearlike
24. *vitreous* — glass-like
25. *wizened* — withered

KEYS TO THE VOCABULARY TESTS

KEY TO VOCABULARY TEST NO. 9.

1. *arbiter* — judge
2. *asperity* — severity
3. *assuaged* — lessened
4. *bellicose* — warlike
5. *candid* — impartial
6. *capricious* — changeable
7. *captious* — faultfinding
8. *caravel* — sailing vessel
9. *devious* — winding
10. *diabolical* — fiendish
11. *enhanced* — raised
12. *gullible* — easily deceived
13. *infamous* — vile
14. *lissom* — lithe
15. *mottled* — spotted
16. *orthographist* — speller
17. *probity* — integrity
18. *reprehension* — censure
19. *strictures* — censures
20. *strident* — shrill
21. *tortuous* — winding
22. *tractable* — easily managed
23. *voracious* — gluttonous
24. *wry* — twisted
25. *xenial* — hospitable

KEY TO VOCABULARY TEST NO. 10.

1. *astringent* — contracting
2. *attrition* — friction
3. *benedicks* — married men
4. *catholic* — liberal
5. *charlatan* — impostor
6. *chicanery* — trickery
7. *chimerical* — visionary
8. *choleric* — hot-tempered
9. *diaphanous* — transparent
10. *diffidence* — shyness
11. *ephemeral* — short-lived
12. *innoxious* — harmless
13. *inveterate* — habitual
14. *littoral* — coastal
15. *mundane* — worldly
16. *otiose* — idle
17. *prognostications* — predictions
18. *renegade* — traitor
19. *replete* — filled
20. *stringent* — severe
21. *succinct* — concise
22. *transient* — short-lived
23. *truculent* — ferocious
24. *vulnerable* — assailable
25. *zenith* — highest point

KEYS TO THE EXERCISES

No keys are supplied for Exercises 15, 17, 35, 59, 97-101, 112, and 113. These omissions are not an oversight. The exercises in question either ask for no answers (15, 17, 35) or would, if supplied with keys, lose their original value (59, 97-101, 112, 113).

Keys To The Exercises

1. A romantic, balmy, enchanting, magnificent tropic night
   A tense, rousing, thrilling football game
   A sturdy, serviceable, stylish, well-constructed pair of shoes
   A well-tailored suit of clothing
   An exquisite, pretty, intelligent, charming child
   A joyous, quiet, restful, enjoyable vacation
   A well-stocked, well-arranged department store
   A fragrant, lathery, good quality cake of soap
   A powerful microscope
   A moving, exquisite, affecting, beautiful poem
   An entertaining moving picture
   An alert, courageous, honest policeman
   A fair, unprejudiced, fearless umpire
   A smart, chic, spruce, becoming, stylish dress
   An astute, capable, able statesman
   Sound, sage, invaluable advice
   An accomplished, talented, competent actress
   A handsome, imposing, beautiful boulevard
   A lilting, catching, haunting, melodious popular tune
   A responsive, quiet, smooth-running typewriter
   A bracing, invigorating sea trip
   A sedulous, efficient, well-trained, courteous, assiduous
   waiter
   A mellow, relaxing, aromatic, tasty cigarette
   A charming, fascinating, delightful, entertaining, stirring,
   thoughtful novel
   A well-delivered, thought-provoking sermon
   Flowing, precise, neat handwriting
   A hilarious, funny, diverting, amusing, entertaining clown
   A sincere, earnest, devoted, benevolent clergyman
   A tuneful, romantic, stirring, moving, splendid opera
   A luxurious, cushioned, comfortable, restful chair
   A shrewd, fortunate, astute purchase on the stock market
   The engaging, charming, winning, endearing personality of
   a friend

131

A just, equitable, fair decision of a jury
The melodious, true, sweet, mellifluous voice of a singer
The sportsmanlike and admirable behavior of some one who
  has been defeated

2. A sultry, oppressive tropic night
A dull, lackadaisical football game
A cheap, ugly pair of shoes
An ill-fitting, cheaply-tailored suit of clothing
An annoying, ill-mannered, impertinent child
A dull, tiring, boring vacation
A poorly arranged department store
A cheap, latherless, adulterated cake of soap
A weak microscope
A prosy, affected poem
A stupid, slow moving picture
A dishonest, timid policeman
An unfair, prejudiced, slow umpire
An unlovely, shapeless, ill-made dress
An obtuse, muddle-headed statesman
Misleading advice
An uninspired, affected, inartistic actress
A narrow, colorless, unsightly boulevard
A cheap, shallow popular tune
A noisy, unresponsive typewriter
A rough, hard sea trip
An idle, discourteous waiter
A cheap, ill-tasting, tasteless cigarette
An obvious, dry, dull, slow, badly plotted, jejune novel
A sleepy, boring, uninspiring, uninspired sermon
Illegible, careless, irregular handwriting
A tiresome clown
An affected, pompous, insincere, worldly, priggish clergyman
A stagey, pretentious, over-wrought opera
An uncomfortable chair
An ill-advised purchase on the stock market
The irritating personality of a friend

The unjust, ill-considered, outrageous decision of a jury
The harsh, untrained, coarse, colorless voice of a singer
The unsportsmanlike, graceless, childish behavior of some one
who has been defeated

3. (a) warm clothing
(b) clothes, costume
(c) it is interesting to compare . . .
(d) lever, instrument, knob
(e) string, ribbon
(f) weakness, fault
(g) ship
(h) visor
(i) article
(j) practice
(k) tool

4. (a) demands (b) needs (c) use (d) requires

5. Astute and shrewd Napoleon; farsighted, sagacious Lincoln; wise, discerning Jefferson; keen-witted Disraeli; the profound Shakespeare; sly, amusing, waggish Groucho Marx; the learned, profoundly intellectual Einstein; a quick, dexterous, adroit acrobat; a skillful, sharp, sly counterfeiter; the keen-witted, diverting Lewis Carroll; a deft, capable, expert waiter; a skillful card-sharper; an inventive and imaginative carpenter.

6. (a) childish, puerile, juvenile; opulent, wealthy, affluent; penniless, destitute; impassive, inactive, indolent
(b) Exhausted; terse, brief; soundless; moronic, imbecilic
(c) Precipitous; adroit; arduous; glittering
(d) Rare, singular; ludicrous; hazardous, perilous; powerful, mighty
(e) Urbane, gallant, obsequious; copious; depressed; gay
(f) Beautiful; forbearing; absurd; iniquitous
(g) Agonizing; mulish; sombre, black; dapper, trim, spruce
(h) Inexplicable, unfathomable; dejected; still, soundless; expansive

(i) Beneficent, benevolent; glassy, sleek; meticulous; dripping, sopping, saturated

(j) Dilatory; profound; speedy; boring, leaden, dingy

(k) Eager; sanguine, confident; haughty, puffed up; scrupulous

7. (a) reach the library, borrow a book for me (b) Buy (c) rent (d) reach (e) earns, or receives (f) persuade (g) earned or took (h) arrive at (i) become, or grow (j) He tires easily (k) grew (l) obtaining; or keep *getting* (m) Get (n) gets (o) growing (p) grows . . , . . . builds . . . , becomes . . , he achieves . . . . (q) . . . became . . . , ... received . . . . (r) find or live in (s) receives (t) was (u) fetch

8. (a) astonished (b) overwhelmed (c) amazed, or overcome (d) It was the professor who was taken by surprise by his wife; no one took the professor's wife by surprise.

9. (a) desire, covet (b) needed (c) covet (d) hoped to (e) were eager to, or were bent upon arriving, or set their hearts on arriving

10. (a) pleased (b) overjoyed (c) delighted (d) happy (e) willing (f) I regret that . . . . (g) upset, worried, displeased, or chagrined (h) distressed over, pained by, upset by, horrified by, or concerned over (i) we regretted our . . . (j) repentant of (k) contrite, or repentant about (l) distressed, unhappy

11. He had an elegant taste in wines.

A painter must have a nice eye for subtle differences in color.

They bought a gorgeous painting by the colorful Turner.

In the opera-house in Paris there is a grand marble staircase.

We propose to erect a great monument to those who died in the Great War.

This roadway is slick with oil.

As a balloon rises into the upper strata, it tends to swell.

The old woman, having spent a lifetime in protecting her own petty interests, had grown clever and cute (rare).

The development from cocoon to butterfly is marvelous.

We expect to see a splendid display of fireworks.

He recognizes the wonderful progress of science in the last fifty years.

His sense of humor is fine, not coarse.

It was a magnificent coronation ceremony.

Blake had a sense of the awful presence of God.

He underwent a horrible experience in shipwreck.

War, once little more than a chivalrous contest, is now terrible.

He pretended to have had a frightful experience with a ghost.

There was a terrific noise of drums which shattered the quiet of the afternoon.

The hero of this book has a fierce, cruel nature.

12. (a) enjoyable . . pleasant . . attractive.
    (b) *gorgeous* is the correct word; so is *nice*.
    (c) exciting
    (d) highly persuasive

13. (a) He is a pleasant fellow, and his wife is delightful; . . . . . . , which is charming.
    (b) It was hot . .
    (c) most agreeable.

14. (a) amused me to see . . . angry (b) slow-witted . . . unpleasant

16. (a) I suppose . . . is attractive, . . he is unpleasant.
    (b) . . are admirable, . . . are impressive.
    (c) suppose . . . repair . . . would need
    (d) replied, maintained, or asserted.
    (e) undertaking

18. (a) We think . . , . . a rather good chance
    (b) She swept
    (c) Human beings can outdistance others . . . will begin at . . . important people.
    (d) Since I am opposed to any . . . , I am joining . . . of about ten thousand

19. *Novel, recent, fresh, young, virgin, unused, fledgling, late, modern, new-born, new-fangled, unfledged.* There are fewer synonyms of *new* than of *old* for the obvious reason that the period of time during which something may be called new is much shorter than the extensive backward reaches of time in which an object may be called old. Something that existed ten thousand years ago may be old as well as something which existed or which began last year. We need many synonyms for *old* in order to differentiate among the manifold different degrees of oldness.

Up-to-the-minute is an adjective expressing a high degree of newness and will stand at the top of your list; *recent* and *modern* are applicable to events that occurred at a considerable remove from the present. Art and literature of fifty years ago are termed modern art and modern literature. *Late*, together with *recent* and *modern*, will stand at the bottom of your list.

20. Ecstatic, transported, entranced, enraptured, jubilant, enchanted, blissful, overjoyed, gleeful, elated, gay, joyful, blithe, rejoicing, sunny, jocund, jovial, jolly, light-hearted, cheerful, cheery, pleased, gladsome, happy, not sorry. This is not an exhaustive list of the many synonyms of *happy*, nor is the order of words beyond criticism. Try to find faults with it.

21. Big, large, considerable, great, mighty, towering, huge, giant, immense, gigantic, vast, enormous, monstrous, stupendous, titanic, infinite.

Little, small, puny, pigmy, dwarfish, tiny, miniature, diminutive, inconsiderable, minute, microscopic, atomic, infinitesimal.

22. (a) *Jaunt, ramble, outing are short; journey, tour, voyage, pilgrimage, expedition* are long.

(b) *Pilgrimage, expedition.*

(c) *Jaunt, ramble, outing.*

(d) *Trip, voyage, excursion;* all excepting *voyage* and *flight* may be used of trips on land.

(e) Voyage; jaunt, ramble, outing.

(f) Ramble

(g) Flight

23. (a) Fragrance, aroma, redolence, perfume, bouquet, scent; fetor, stench, stink, fetidness

(b) Smell, odor

(c) Fragrance or aroma; fetor or stench

(d) Stink

24. Beauteous, beautiful, lovely, handsome, personable, comely, fair, good-looking, pretty, well-favored.

(a) None of these adjectives can properly be applied to an automobile, a building, or a house.

(b) Beautiful

(c) Beautiful or pretty

25. The following groups of adjectives are *not* arranged in progressive order; it seems best to leave such arrangement to the individual student:

Ugly, plain, homely, inartistic, unsightly, uncomely, coarse, unprepossessing, ill-favored, uncouth, gross, hideous, repellent, repulsive.

Stingy, parsimonious, penurious, miserly, mean, near, niggardly, close, tight-fisted.

Neat, ship-shape, tidy, orderly, trim, dapper, natty.

Timid, fearful, shy, afraid, timorous, diffident, faint-hearted, apprehensive, chicken-hearted,

Brave, courageous, bold, valiant, valorous, gallant, intrepid, spirited, mettlesome, plucky, stout-hearted, daring, audacious, dauntless, venturesome.

Polite, courteous, urbane, civil, mannerly, well-mannered, well-behaved, polished, refined, chivalrous, suave, ingratiating, cordial, gracious.

Soft, supple, tender, pliable, pliant, flexible, downy, malleable, plastic, ductile, tractable, yielding, flaccid.

Hard, rigid, stiff, firm, unyielding, inflexible, adamant, stony, rocky, bony; difficult, laborious, onerous, arduous, formidable.

Careful, prudent, heedful, regardful, cautious, considerate, provident, watchful, accurate, exact.

Little, tiny, small, minute, pigmy, molecular, microscopic, diminutive.

Far, distant, removed, remote, inaccessible.

Heavy, ponderous, weighty, cumbersome, burdensome, unwieldy, massive.

Strong, powerful, mighty, vigorous, potent, forcible, virile, brawny, sinewy, strapping, stalwart, muscular, Herculean, sturdy, robust.

Weak, feeble, impotent, defenseless, infirm, faint, flimsy, frail, fragile.

Imprudent, neglecting, unmindful, negligent, careless, thoughtless, unwary, unwatchful, reckless, improvident.

26. (a) Walk, march, step along, pace, plod, trudge, tramp, stalk, stride, toddle, jog on

(b) Speed, stream, sweep along; drift

(c) Move, go, pass, glide, flow, run

(d) A dirigible glides; a horse plods, walks, trots, or gallops; an automobile runs or speeds; a rowboat moves, drifts, or glides along; a bullet speeds; a current of air flows or streams; a runner sweeps along, runs, jogs, or strides; and a shadow passes or glides.

27. In addition to those words listed, the following are often useful: represent, advance, propose, propound, enunciate, broach, contend, pronounce, avow, asseverate, express, deliver, blurt, talk, hold forth, harangue, spout, rant, recite, lecture, preach, discourse, expatiate, tell, inform, soliloquize, chatter, prattle, prate, jabber, gush, ask, inquire, question, interrogate, answer, reply, respond.

28. (a) No. (b) One would try to sharpen a pencil. To endeavor implies the exertion of considerable effort against opposition. If, for instance, some one were trying to take the pencil or the knife away from the sharpener, then he might well say that he was endeavoring to sharpen the pencil.

(c) When one essays to do something, he does not try very hard; he is, as it were, merely testing his powers.

(d) *To strive*

(e) *To undertake*

(f) One strives to escape from prison, endeavors to defeat a competitor of equal or slightly more than equal strength, attempts a task of some difficulty, undertakes to accomplish something which he has often accomplished successfully, and essays to write a novel which he thinks he has the ability to write.

29. (a) vanquished, defeated
    (b) subjecting, quelling, or subduing
    (c) defeated, put down
    (d) routed

30. *Necromancer, wizard, seer, sorcerer, magician, conjurer, witch, diviner, soothsayer, enchanter, medium, clairvoyant, exorcist, thaumaturgist,* and *sibyl* are some of the more common. A witch is a female who practices the black art of dealing with evil spirits in order to work harm upon human beings. A wizard is a male witch. A sorcerer employs supernatural agencies, usually evil. A magician is an expert in the arts of magic; popularly he is a prestidigitator. A conjuror is either a juggling artist in sleight-of-hand or one who employs genuinely supernatural arts. A necromancer is one who prophecies by means of pretended communication with the dead. A seer, as his name implies, sees into the future and is consequently the same as a prophet. A thaumaturgist works miracles. An enchanter is one who exerts a magic spell (originally with the aid of song) upon any one or anything. A diviner foretells the future by supernatural aid. A medium is one who is believed to be controlled by the spirit of a dead person. A clairvoyant is a clear-seeing person who, often in a trance, can perceive things not visible to ordinary persons. An exorcist can call up and drive out evil spirits, usually by some formula or ceremony. A soothsayer is a truth-speaker who claims unusual insight.

31. (a) *Letting* is the general word, implying nothing about the state of mind of the person who lets another drive his automobile. *Tolerating* the driving of one's automobile suggests that one does not altogether like the idea. *Suffering* implies even greater dislike. One *agrees to* such use after some discussion. When one authorizes the use of his automobile, he gives formal permission. To vouchsafe the privilege implies a degree of condescension.

32. (a) Wit is more intellectual than humor. Wit arises from the play of ideas or words, humor from actions. A clever pun is an example of wit; any funny action appeals to the sense of humor.

(b) A scheme implies a shrewdness in its concoction that is lacking in the idea of a plan. One would speak of a plan to build a cathedral, not a scheme; but a fraudulent stock would be sold to the public by a scheme, not a plan.

(c) *Tool* is a word of narrower application than *instrument*; *tool* is restricted to the workshop and the factory, but phonographs, pianos, microscopes, surgical knives, X-ray machines, and other devices of considerable precision are called instruments. Instrument is always the word for the tools used by scientists in their pursuits.

(d) *Shop* is the English word, *store* the American. In the United States *shop* is applied to small stores and carries with it a suggestion of some elegance.

(e) *Advice* suggests that the adviser is superior, or considers himself at least momentarily superior, to the advisee. *Counsel* implies equality between the two. One gives advice to a small boy, counsel to one's intimate friend.

(f) A trophy is a token of victory over an enemy, taken from the enemy by the victor. *Souvenir* and *memento* are almost indistinguishable, but a memento is retained more for the purpose of reminding one of some event or place than is a souvenir. The origin of a souvenir may be more easily forgotten than that of a memento.

(g) A jail is a house of detention for those suspected of, or guilty of, comparatively minor offenses. A prison is for more serious offenders. A jail is likely to be under local auspices, a prison under state or national control.

(h) To pilfer is to commit a petty theft; to thieve is more serious. *To steal* is the general term, with few implications; one can steal a dollar or a hundred thousand dollars. *To purloin* stresses the idea of the removal of a stolen article. *To appropriate* suggests that one takes another's property for one's own use.

(i) *Liking* is the least intense of the three words. Affection implies some warmth of feeling; love is the most fervent of the three.

(j) Something is absurd if it violates all the laws of reason. Something silly is more contemptible than it is amusing. That which is ridiculous stimulates laughter; so does the laughable; but the ridiculous is far more absurd and unreasonable than the laughable, which is merely funny enough to arouse laughter.

(k) A good pun is wit. Any play on words is basically intellectual and therefore better called wit than humor.

(l) He would speak of a plan. He might also use the words *project, program,* or *measure.*

(m) A surgical tool would be an instrument without the requisite delicacy and precision.

(n) Prison.

(o) No. Pilfering implies pettiness in the theft.

(p) Funny, ridiculous, laughable. *Funny* implies that people would be laughing with you or at you with your approval; laughable suggests that people would be amused at you because of peculiarities or actions beyond your control.

33. (a) momentary (b) fugitive, fleeting, transient, ephemeral (c) ephemeral, short-lived (d) flying, flitting (e) evanescent (f) temporary, short, momentary (g) passing (h) short-lived

34. (a) interminable, timeless (b) undying, eternal, deathless, imperishable, everlasting, everliving, unfading, fadeless, and immortal. *Timeless* suggests to a purist that Lincoln was famous before his birth, even ten thousand years ago. *Incessant, ceaseless, unceasing,* and *continual* would be inappropriate because they emphasize the idea that no pause intervenes; whereas one speaking about the fame of Lincoln would doubtless wish to emphasize the length of duration of Lincoln's fame rather than its steadiness.
(c) perennial, undying, eternal, imperishable, ever-living, unfading, fadeless, immortal, and timeless.
(d) incessant, interminable
(e) interminable, endless
(f) undying.

36. (a) took off, aped, or mimicked . . . , . . . emulate
(b) imitate
(c) follows, borrows from
(d) imitate
(e) copies, imitates, apes
(f) *To parody* something is to retain the style of the original but to treat of another subject in that style. *To travesty* is to treat the same subject-matter in a different style. *To burlesque* is merely to imitate something, perhaps very loosely but with sufficient resemblance to recall the original. It one were to write of a baseball game in the style of *Paradise Lost,* that would be a parody. If one were to deal with the subject-matter of *Paradise Lost* in the style of a nursery-rhyme, that would be a travesty. If one were to put on the airs of a pompous friend and were to do it well enough to ensure recognition of one's intention, that would be a burlesque.

37. (1) Enthusiasm: zeal, ecstasy, excitement, fanaticism, **fervency,** rapture, fervor, frenzy, transport, inspiration, passion

(2) Imagination: phantasy, fancy

(3) Impudence: effrontery, pertness, forwardness, rudeness, impertinence, incivility, insolence

(4) Name: title, cognomen, epithet

(5) Mob: canaille, rabble, populace

(6) Necessity: exigency, extremity, requisite, urgency

38. (a) Carriage, car, chaise, coach, chariot, automobile, victoria, diligence, stage, cab, bicycle, velocipede, train, balloon, roadster

(b) Cart, dray, truck, barrow, lorry

(c) Carriage, wagon, coach, dray, landau, equipage, cart

(d) Truck, automobile, motorcycle, motor car, bus

(e) Ox-cart, pony-cart; but not dog-cart (drawn by a horse)

(f) Sled, sledge, cutter, sleigh, toboggan, bobsled

(g) Bicycle, Tricycle, monocycle, tandem, motorcycle, velocipede, wheelbarrow

(h) Freight car, Pullman car, baggage car, etc.

39. Sad, clumsy, ugly, learned, leisurely, distant

40. Encouraged, rested, rational, compulsory, recondite, contemptible.

41. Deceitful, abyss, malevolent, feeble, unwholesome.

42. None of these words has an exact antonym excepting possibly *blemish*, whose antonym, in some senses and contexts, would be *virtue*.

43. Antonyms of *fool, dapper, cooperate,* and *rival* are *sage, slovenly, hinder, ally. Faultless,* implying merely an absence of fault, without, necessarily, the presence of any virtue, has no precise antonym; *property* seems to have no precise antonym, there being no name for that which is not property. There is no antonym of *senator;* that is, there is no noun applicable to a person who is the opposite of a senator, nor, strictly speaking, is there such a person.

44. Combination, decomposition.
Copy, prototype
Sequence, precedence
Dispersion, recall
Plurality, fraction
Irregularity, periodicity
Continuance, cessation
Paternity, posterity
Energy, quiescence
Interval, contiguity, continuity
Support, pendency
Distortion, symmetry
Impulse, recoil
Gravity, levity
Motion, quiescence

45. (a) indolence (b) solemnity (c) rashness

46. *Commerce, harness, property, pecuniary,* and *January* clearly have no antonyms; nothing exists, for instance, which is the precise opposite of harness, and as a consequence no word exists for the expression of such an idea. The opposite of *crew* may be considered to be *passengers;* of *knight, peasant* or *villain;* of *revelry, asceticism;* of *circumference, center;* of *collision, recoil,* of *duty, dereliction;* and of *round,* possibly *square.*

47. adversity, prosperity
loss, gain
receipt, payment
seclusion, publicity
contempt, admiration
oblivion, remembrance
truth, falsehood
shortcoming, virtue

plunge, leap
orthodoxy, heterodoxy
condemnation, praise
jealousy, sympathy
ambush, exposure
summit, base
holy, profane

48. foolish, sensible
latent, active

taciturn, garrulous
extemporaneous, premeditated

permanent, temporary
stable, variable
sullen, joyous
deep, shallow
sensual, spiritual
pensive, blithe
idiotic, intelligent
professional, amateur
professional, undergraduate

significant, meaningless
proficient, unskilled
secure, perilous
indefensible, pardonable
tenacious, irresolute
liberal, parsimonious
favorite, most disliked

49. regret, be reconciled to
believe, doubt
aspire, despond
serve, hinder
hurtle, balk
degenerate, improve
condense, expand
deplore, approve
withdraw, enter
hum, click
dawn, darken
cure, injure
possess, discard

amuse, irritate
shout, whisper
ingratiate, provoke dislike
sicken, convalesce
speed, retard
humiliate, elevate
glower, smile
praise, blame
bless, curse
glorify, degrade
stagger, glide
anger, placate

50. fame, oblivion
thoroughfare, blind alley
circumspection, thoughtlessness
taciturnity, garrulity
mercy, pitilessness
erudition, ignorance
rectitude, perfidy
chaos, order

scholar, teacher
docility, stubbornness
squalor, cleanliness
veracity, falseness
innuendo, statement
axiom, nonsense
flattery, insult

51. restive, quiet
tentative, established
propitious, unlucky
deficient, sufficient
eager, loath

rebellious, loyal
reluctant, avid
prejudiced, open-minded
fractious, good-tempered
fictitious, actual

lewd, pure
auxiliary, obstructive
physical, spiritual

bizarre, common
precarious, safe
native, foreign

52. teach, learn
quit, continue
warn, tempt
attack, defend
defend, assail
fail, triumph
obey, defy
permit, forbid

offer, decline
promise, refuse
gain, lose
give, take
lend, borrow
hope, despair
confess, deny

53. learn, instruct
persevere, give up
tempt, dissuade
reject, accept
succeed, fail
disobey, comply
forbid, allow
refuse, agree

deny, admit
lose, gain
sell, buy
borrow, advance
receive, give
keep, give
laugh, weep

54. go forward: advance, proceed, progress, go ahead, recoil
        recede, return, withdraw, revert
    go up: ascend, climb, mount, rise
        descend, drop, fall, gravitate, settle, sink, decline
    arrive: reach, get to, land, attain, disembark
        depart, leave, vacate, quit
    appear: materialize, become visible, seem, look
        disappear, vanish, dissolve, fade away, be effaced
    ask: request, question, inquire, demand
        answer, reply, respond, retort, explain
    remember: recollect, recall, keep in mind, call up
        forget, escape the mind, escape recall, unlearn
    amuse: divert, entertain, cheer, tickle, titillate
        annoy, irritate, bore, weary, tire, disgust
    conceal: hide, cover, secrete, screen, cloak, shroud, veil
        impart, make known, communicate, announce, disclose

55. dislike: hate, abhor, detest, contemn, despise
　　　like, love, admire, cherish, dote upon
take: carry, receive, transport, convey, remove
　　　give, donate, offer, hand to, tender
open: unlock, uncover, unseal, unfold, release
　　　shut, close, cover, seal, enclose
win: succeed, attain, gain, earn, achieve
　　　lose, fail, forfeit, miss, be deprived of
praise: laud, eulogize, commend, acclaim, compliment
　　　blame, abuse, censure, condemn, disparage
help: aid, assist, succor, relieve, abet
　　　hinder, prevent, stop, burden, impede
begin: commence, set out, start, institute, inaugurate
　　　end, finish, cease, stop, conclude
labor: work, drudge, toil, slave, travail
　　　idle, loaf, loll about, lounge, loiter
live: dwell, exist, subsist, abide, survive
　　　die, expire, decline, perish, wither
join: connect, combine, unite, associate, conjoin
　　　separate, sunder, cleave, disconnect, dissever
fall: drop, decline, sink, fail, subside
　　　rise, climb, ascend, mount, soar
eat: devour, munch, consume, feed upon, chew
　　　fast, starve, abstain, famish, hunger

56. wrong: erroneous, incorrect, faulty, amiss
　　　right, correct, proper, fitting, accurate
smooth: level, polished, even, sleek, glossy, silken, glassy
　　　rough, uneven, rugged, gnarled, jagged
generous: liberal, bountiful, unsparing, open-handed
　　　saving, chary, parsimonious, penurious, stingy
first: initial, initiatory, inceptive, inaugural, primary
　　　last, final, terminal, conclusive, ultimate
young: youthful, juvenile, unfledged, callow
　　　old, aged, elderly, senile, decrepit, patriarchal
slow: slack, gradual, sluggish, languid
　　　fast, quick, hurried, speedy, swift, rapid, fleet

soft: tender, pliant, flexible, yielding, flabby
    hard, rigid, stiff, firm, adamantine, callous
wide: broad, ample, outspread, extended, extensive
    narrow, thin, spare, contracted, lank
alike: similar, resembling, like, twin, analogous, parallel
    unalike, dissimilar, different, disparate, divergent
empty: void, vacant, unoccupied, deserted, devoid
    full, pervaded, saturated, filled, packed, stuffed
sweet: sugary, candied, honied, saccharine, cloying
    sour, tart, acid, green, acidulous
thick: broad, wide, thickset
    thin, narrow, constricted, slender, fine, slim, spare
stupid: unintelligent, mindless, witless, dull, bovine
    keen, clever, brilliant, intellectual, intelligent
wet: moist, damp, saturated, humid, dank, muggy
    dry, waterless, sear, desiccated, anhydrous
loud: noisy, blatant, clangorous, deafening, ear-splitting
    faint, low, gentle, whispered, dulcet
short: brief, compact, curt, abbreviated
    long, elongated, lengthy, stretched out, interminable
open: unclosed, ajar, agape, perforated, pervious
    closed, shut, sealed, unopened, impenetrable
sad: sorry, unhappy, depressed, grieved, cheerless, downcast
    cheerful, happy, gay, blithe, elated, buoyant
difficult: hard, irksome, laborious, onerous, arduous
    easy, simple, facile, light
optimistic: hopeful, sanguine, confident, fearless
    pessimistic, fearful, timorous, apprehensive

57. beginning: start, commencement, opening, outset
    end, close, termination, conclusion, finish
man: male, gentleman, master, fellow, mankind
    woman, female, lady, girl, matron
knowledge: familiarity, comprehension, learning, erudition
    ignorance, nescience, unacquaintance
danger: peril, insecurity, jeopardy, risk, hazard
    safety, security, impregnability, lack of danger

front: face, foreground, frontage, facade, frontispiece
    back, rear, posterior, background, stern
top: peak, summit, apex, vertex, zenith, pinnacle, acme
    bottom, base, foot, basement, foundation, nadir
care: precaution, solicitude, heed, heedfulness, scruple
    neglect, carelessness, improvidence, negligence
warning: premonition, caution, notice, admonition
    inducement, seduction, temptation, enticement
youth: infancy, adolescence, immaturity
    age, oldness, senility, decrepitude, dotage
pleasure: delight, hedonism, diversion, gratification
    pain, suffering, agony, torment, torture
wisdom: sagacity, understanding, acumen, penetration
    folly, imbecility, foolishness, stupidity, puerility
friend: comrade, companion, partner, intimate, associate, chum
    enemy, foe, opponent, antagonist
life: vitality, animation, vivacity, existence
    death, dying, decease, demise, dissolution
outside: exterior, surface, skin, covering
    inside, interior, contents, substance, heart
good: benefit, advantage, interest, virtue, blessing, prosperity
    bad, evil, ill, wickedness, harm, mischief, disaster
war: conflict, carnage, warfare, hostilities, fighting, battle
    peace, conciliation, amnesty, terms, truce, armistice
cause: origin, source, causation, genesis, influence, reason
    effect, consequence, result, upshot, issue, outcome
sound: noise, tone, resonance, voice, racket
    silence, stillness, quiet, hush, peace, muteness
health: soundness, vigor, wholesomeness
    disease, sickness, illness, infirmity, malady, ailment
master: lord, captain, commander, chief, leader, ruler
    servant, slave, subject, henchman, follower, menial

58. short: abbreviated, terse, brief, transient
    long, attenuated, lengthy
sharp: acute, pointed, edged, keen, piercing, cutting
    dull, blunt, obtuse, bluff

enough: sufficient, plenty, ample
    insufficient, scant, inadequate
possible: practicable, feasible, workable, achievable
    impossible, hopeless, impracticable, unworkable
clean: immaculate, unsoiled, unsullied, spotless
    dirty, sullied, filthy, grimy, soiled, fouled
strong: powerful, muscular, potent, vigorous, robust
    weak, feeble, frail, fragile, debilitated
heavy: ponderous, weighty, oppressive, cumbersome
    light, buoyant, volatile, lively
lazy: indolent, slothful, sluggish, idle
    active, energetic, vital, assiduous
sane: rational, lucid, well-balanced, sound
    insane, crazy, idiotic, demented, deranged
useful: beneficial, profitable, serviceable, aiding
    hindering, futile, fruitless, worthless, profitless
high: raised, elevated, lofty, eminent, exalted, towering
    low, base, deep, sunk, degraded, depressed
hot: burning, warm, heated, torrid, fervid, roasting
    cold, cool, chilly, frigid, icy, freezing, biting
dark: gloomy, obscure, shady, murky, sombre
    light, shining, luminous, lucid, lucent, bright, vivid
cheap: inexpensive, reasonable, gratuitous
    expensive, costly, dear, high, precious, exorbitant
free: liberated, adrift, gratuitous, complimentary
    imprisoned, subject, enslaved, costly
curved: bent, rounded, devious, bowed, vaulted, semi-circular
    straight, direct, true, unbent, undeviating
plain: simple, unadorned, ugly, homely
    complicated, ornamented, ornate, rich, fancy
loud: noisy, raucous, obstreperous, boisterous, blatant, deafening
    faint, inaudible, low, muffled, gentle, soft, whispered
clear: lucid, transparent, limpid, vitreous, crystalline
    opaque, turbid, muddy, obfuscated
important: momentous, weighty, salient, memorable, serious
    trivial, unimportant, trifling, paltry, frivolous
convex: protuberant, projecting, salient
    concave, cup-shaped, depressed, hollow, scooped out

willing: eager, inclined, compliant, agreeable, fain, disposed
    unwilling, loath, reluctant, grudging, disinclined
visible: perceptible, discernible, apparent, obvious, clear
    invisible, imperceptible, indiscernible
true: veracious, scrupulous, accurate, actual, veritable, correct
    false, mendacious, erroneous, fallacious, groundless

60. A circular staircase is one which rises steadily in the shape of a helix; or it is a staircase rotating about an imaginary axis and rising from the floor at an even rate of progression.

61. The definitions here and in the following sections have been made by students. They are all reasonably accurate and acceptable but leave room in most cases for improvement.

(a) A friend is a person who is attached to one by loyalty, affection, and esteem and with whom one may be completely sincere and natural.

(b) A wheelbarrow is a small cart for the conveyance of material; it has at one end a single wheel and at the other two handles by which that end may be supported and by which the barrow may be pushed or pulled along.

(c) An automobile is a vehicle designed for the conveyance of passengers; it is usually a four-wheeled machine propelled by a gasoline-engine and operated from one of the forward seats.

(d) A clergyman is a man sworn to the service of God and of the Episcopal or English Church.

(e) A book is a group of printed sheets of the same size bound together in order and protected by a cover.

(f) A prejudice is a belief so strongly held that it cannot be shaken by argument or reason.

62. (a) To boil is to raise a liquid by heat to the point where it is agitated by escaping gases.

(b) To laugh is to make a noise with the vocal organs in such a way as to show joy, merriment, contempt, or amusement.

(c) To run is to progress by a regular series of alternate steps with the feet in such a way that both feet are momentarily off the ground together for a part of each step.

(d) To walk is to advance comparatively slowly by a series of alternate steps, raising the rear foot from the ground at the same instant that the front foot is set on the ground.

(e) To gamble is to engage oneself in a game or a situation in which one trusts to luck that the outcome will be favorable to him.

(f) To yawn is to open the mouth to its fullest or almost its fullest extent in order to inhale an unusually large draught of air; yawning habitually occurs in moments of fatigue, sleepiness, or boredom.

(g) To ascertain is to discover by inquiry or investigation.

63. (a) *zigzag* is an adjective descriptive of a line which is composed of straight sections frequently changing direction.

(b) *beautiful*: pleasing to one's sense of symmetry, grace, and harmony.

(c) *plump*: somewhat fat. The word has a slight humorous implication.

(d) *early*: occurring sooner than is usual; or occurring among the first events in a series.

(e) *disgusting*: arousing strong disapproval based chiefly upon taste.

(f) *sporadic*: occurring at irregular intervals.

(g) *continual*: recurring at regular intervals for a considerable period of time.

64. (a) To trot is to progress at a gait between a walk and a run. The action is remarkable for the slight up-and-down motion which accompanies it. The word applies especially to horses.

(b) To expostulate is to object strongly to some action of another, adducing reasons for one's objection.

(c) To remonstrate is to protest, adducing reasons. *Remonstrate* implies greater severity than does *expostulate*.

(d) To wrestle is to engage in a grappling contest with another.

(e) To vote is to indicate one's opinion, in common with others, on some issue in such a way that the opinion will be counted equally with the opinion of each of the others.

(f) To listen is to make use of that one of the senses which has the function of perceiving sound.

(g) To hope is to have a desire with some expectation of obtaining that desire.

65. (a) A bog is an area of water-saturated ground which is too wet and soft to sustain the weight of a heavy body placed upon it.

(b) A school is an educational institution where persons, especially the young, are taught various branches of study, especially the rudiments of knowledge.

(c) The sky is the upper region of our atmosphere and that which lies beyond. It presents the appearance of being a blue arch.

(d) A king is the supreme ruler of a real or nominal monarchy.

(e) A wharf is a man-made projection, consisting usually of wood or concrete supported on piles, extending from the land into the water, and usually designed for the purpose of loading and unloading ships and boats.

66. (a) A dog is a meat-eating, domesticated, intelligent mammal which demonstrates a remarkable capacity for loyalty to mankind.

(b) A floor is the inside, flat, level, bottom surface of an enclosed space such as a room.

(c) A door is a surface, usually flat and rectangular, used to close the entrance to any walled-in area. It is usually hinged, or designed to slide back and forth or up and down in such a way as to open and close the entrance.

(d) A yacht is a pleasure craft of some size usually privately owned. It is ordinarily powered by sail, steam, or motor and has cabin space designed for the comfortable accommodation of a group of people.

(e) A shovel is a tool used for the lifting and conveyance of any comparatively loose material. It consists of a longish handle at the end of which is attached firmly a flat or slightly curved blade so designed as to make the shovel perform its function with the greatest possible efficiency.

67. (a) A bicycle is a vehicle remarkable for the fact that its two wheels are mounted one behind the other. Because of its design it must be balanced by its rider while in motion. Power is supplied by the pressure of the rider's feet upon pedals so designed as to convey the power to the rear wheel.

(b) A knee is the joint in a leg approximately midway between the hip and the ankle.

(c) Murder is the wilful and criminal slaying of one person by another.

(d) A pyramid is a geometric structure square at the base and with four sides rising in triangular form to meet conjointly at an apex. Or a pyramid is a conical structure consisting of five sides, one of which is square and is called the base, and the other four of which are triangular, usually equilateral.

(e) A triangle is a three-sided plane.

(f) Embarrassment is discomposure resulting from a feeling of inferiority in some social situation.

68. (a) A saddle is a seat, usually made of leather, which makes riding a horse more comfortable and easy. It is fastened to the back of the horse by a strap or girth which passes under the horse's stomach.

(b) Indescribable: not capable of being pictured or characterized in human language.

(c) Oval: elliptical or egg-shaped; oblong with rounded ends.

(d) A gentleman is a man who is well-bred, well-behaved, honorable, and courteous.

(e) A relic is a comparatively small portion remaining from that which has long since vanished or been destroyed.

(f) *Square* means having a figure that possesses four right angles and four equal sides, all of them lying upon a plane.

(g) *Sickly*: habitually in poor health.

(h) *Pink*: the color which results from a more or less equal mixture of red and white pigments.

TWELVE WAYS TO BUILD A VOCABULARY

(i) *Solemn*: arousing serious thought; or marked by seriousness and gravity of demeanor.

(j) A banquet is an elaborate feast.

(k) A fish is an aquatic creature with a backbone, gills, scales, and fins.

(l) A smile is an expression on the face marked by an up-turning of the corners of the mouth and some squinting of the eyes, and suggestive of pleasure or amusement.

69. (a) extricate, incontrovertible
    (b) misanthrope
    (c) prodigy
    (d) geography, contiguous
    (e) orthography
    (f) superfluous
    (g) benevolence (?)
    (h) intellectual
    (i) proposition
    (j) intercepted
    (k) influence

70. (a) precipitate
    (b) particulars
    (c) catastrophe
    (d) caparison
    (e) ingenuous
    (f) tuition
    (g) ineligible
    (h) ineffable
    (i) implications

71. (a) contemptible
    (b) masterly
    (c) deprecate
    (d) alternative
    (e) regrettable
    (f) precipitate
    (g) forcible
    (h) luxuriant
    (i) predict
    (j) proceed
    (k) analyze
    (l) legislature

72. (a) yearly; occurring every two years; occurring every three years; continuing through the year or for many years; history

described year by year; to incapacitate on account of age (years).

(b) rhythm as it falls more or less regularly; a falling away from some standard; falling off (of leaves); the west, where the sun falls before one.

(c) a cut or break in the middle of a poetic line or foot; a cutting out.

(d) not hot (not enthusiastic); pertaining to heat; units of heat.

(e) openness or shining-ness of personality; frank, with truth shining through; made shining or luminous by heat; one who shines in a white robe, as did Roman candidates for office; maliciously setting on fire (causing to shine!).

(f) melodious, singing; hymn; division of a poem (poetry being associated intimately with music); to charm (by singing); magic spell (induced by singing); leader of the musical part of a service of worship.

(g) fleshly; flesh-eating; being made into flesh.

(h) a chain-like series; like a chain.

(i) one-hundredth anniversary; having to do with a one-hundredth anniversary; having one hundred steps; having one hundred feet; captain of (originally) a troop of one hundred soldiers.

(j) growing (into a full circle); something which has grown out from another body; an enlargement, or a "growing-into"; a decrease, or a "growing away from."

73. (a) a section of a dormitory where one lies down to sleep; to sit or lie upon in order to hatch; a discouraging and hampering load that lies upon one.

(b) careful; a rector's assistant who cares for certain details of the activities of the church; a Roman administrator who was given charge or care over a province; without care or worry; a position with few duties or cares.

(c) one of a body of ten men; occurring every ten years, or lasting ten years; to kill one out of every ten; a period of ten years.

(d) something "said out", a decree; to "say in", or to charge with crime.

(e) to lead out the powers in one; to lead some one into doing something; to induce in addition; a leader of the aristocracy, a noblewoman of highest rank; to lead together or contribute to.

(f) pertaining to marriage (pertaining to those joined together), a group of men joined together in a faction.

(g) some one sent as a representative from; to send back.

(h) related on the father's side ("born to"); related ("born together"); inherent ("born in"); beginning to be born; of birth.

(i) not harmful; harmful; harmful to.

(j) a surname; disgrace ("no name," in the sense of reputation); list or system of names; in name only; a name together with something else.

74. (a) one quarter of a circle; having four feet; a square dance for four couples; isolation for forty days; company of soldiers drawn up in a square.

(b) extortionate (that is, seizing another's property); seizing of property by superior force; seize with delight

(c) transgress ("come against"); come or meet together; come between; follow closely ("come after").

(d) affirm as true; truthful; prove true; truth; appearance of truth.

(e) one who wears clothing of the other sex; strip (of clothing); clothing of state, robe of clergy; a room for clothing in a church.

(f) turn aside ("from the way"); prevent ("meet in the way") capable of penetration ("the way through"); incapable of penetration; bridge-like structure designed to carry a roadway over a valley.

75. (a) water (b) rough (c) to hear (d) to increase (e) gold

76. (a) head (b) *crucial* means "at the crossroads"; *crucify* means "fix on a cross"; *cruciform* mean "cross-shaped"; and *excruciate* means "cause extreme pain, as if on a cross." (c) fault.

77. (a) upward slope; downward slope; natural slope or tendency toward.

(b) collar (for the neck); one who carries wares hung about his neck (now applied to the agent of a religious society who distributes books, etc.); decapitation (naturally at the neck).

(c) horny part of the eyeball; horny thickness of skin; a little horn; a horn of plenty; an animal with one horn.

(d) a body of people; a dead body; body-ish, fat; a little body; to embody.

(e) believable; a misbeliever (and, by logical extension, a mis-doer); one false to a belief or a cause.

78. domain, demesne, dominate, domineer
durance, duration, endure, obdurate
err, erratum, erroneous, error

exterior, external, extreme, strange
affidavit, confide, fiducial, infidel, perfidious
conflagration, flagrant
affluent, confluence, fluent, fluctuate, fluid, superfluous
facility, facilitate

79. Flock. Flocking together; singled out from the flock for some peculiar characteristic; to flock together; to separate from the flock.

80. (a) to make lighter; to make light by fermentation; lightness, frivolity

(b) not lawful; exceeding the bounds of what is allowed, one allowed to practice a profession

(c) to erase (as a letter); the repetition of a sound (letter) at the beginnings of a series of syllables; actual (in accordance with the letter rather than the spirit)

(d) make longer; long life; longness in an east-west direction

(e) talkativeness; defamatory talk; one who talks from his stomach; monologue ("talk alone"); conversation ("talk with")

(f) to make clear or shining; translucent ("shining through")

(g) saucy (meaning originally "badly expert"); to feign bad health; bad conduct

(h) one who takes dictation by hand; a handcuff; to work with the hands; done by hand; release a slave (send away from one's hand); written by hand; to make by hand

(i) to come between in order to reconcile; pertaining to the middle; concerning the Middle Ages; middling in quality

81. (a) All these words have in common the idea of "please". *Complacent* means pleased with oneself; *placable* means capable of being appeased or pleased; *placid* means calm or serene (because pleased).

(b) All three words contain the idea of "level": an esplanade is a level open space; a pianoforte is an instrument designed to produce both soft (level) and loud tones; a plane is a level surface.

(c) These four words have in common the idea of "fill": an addition which fills up or completes; a word which fills out a place in a sentence which would otherwise appear empty; complete (filled); and completeness.

(d) The idea of "fold" is present in these words: the state of being an accomplice ("folded together"): plainly expressed ("folded outward"); to beseech (to "fold down" or "bend down" to someone in making a request).

(e) The thought of praying is at the root of these words: to deprecate is literally to pray earnestly against; to imprecate is to pray upon someone, that is, to call down a curse (a kind of prayer) upon; and *precarious* means "dangerous" because it means "obtained by prayer or as a favor" and therefore doubtful and uncertain.

(f) The idea of "first" appears in these three words: belonging to the first ages; seniority by virtue of having been born first; the first rose (?).

(g) The idea of "honest" or "good" lies at the heart of both of these words: *approbation* is approval, or the estimation of something as good; probity is honesty or goodness of character.

(h) The thought of fighting is present in these three words: to *impugn*, meaning "to call in question", has a literal meaning of "to fight against"; to oppugn is to oppose or fight against; and pugnacity is a disposition to fight.

(i) The idea of "sacred" is contained in these words: to profane or make unsacred; priestly; violation of anything sacred; a sacred rite; to curse as being not sacred.

82. (a) fitful, leaping from one to the other; elastic, leaping back; leaping

(b) healthful; healthful

(c) to surfeit, to make one feel that he has had enough; to soak thoroughly (enough)

(d) foreknowledge; one who has a smattering of knowledge

(e) heraldic shield; shield-shaped

(f) cut in two; "cut into" (an insect is apparently divided into segments); cut across or through

(g) diligent (setting oneself to a task); do harm by sitting in wait

(h) scatter like seed; a seed-plot of ideas, a school

(i) funeral rites, following upon death; sycophantically following another

(j) make or become like; to pretend to be like something else, to conceal by feigning; to imitate, pretend to be like

(k) sounding; resounding, reverberating

(l) tending to bind organic tissues; binding, rigid, severe

(m) projecting tablet-like frieze or cornice

(n) touching at the edge; perceptible to the touch or other senses

83. (a) Latin, *cover*: a natural outer covering, such as a skin

(b) Latin, *time*: living at the same time; on the spur of the moment

(c) Latin, *hold*: unyielding, holding to one's purpose; ability to hold firmly to one's purpose

(d) Latin, *thin*: to make thin; to minimize ("thin out") the seriousness of a fault

(e) Latin, *rub*: a rubbing away; worn out by repetition

(f) Latin, *twist*: to twist into an unnatural or irregular shape; a private or civil wrong; twisting; a collar of (twisted) wire.

(g) Latin, *three*: a ship with three banks of oars; one of three men who rule together; an ornament in a frieze having three vertical incisions or uprights

(h) Latin, *swell*: a mound; swollen; swelling

(i) Latin, *wave*: flooding, as by waves; to move like a wave

(j) Latin, *health*: a bidding farewell, that is, a saying of "good health!"; one in bad health, one seeking to recover health

(k) Latin, *straddling*: to branch off; to use ambiguous, straddling language

(l) Latin, *live*: festive, jovial, lively together with others; liveliness; dissection of a living animal

(m) Latin, *call*: a diversion calling one away from his vocation; to call forth; to recall; calling out loudly

84. (a) From a Latin word meaning "heavy": to cause sorrow; to make worse or heavier

(b) From a Latin word meaning "friendly": pleasing, agreeable, friendly; showing good will

(c) From a Latin word meaning "to announce": to proclaim; to announce

(d) From a Latin word meaning "price": to set a value upon; to esteem adequately

(e) From Latin words meaning "together" or "like": to bring or come together; to take and incorporate together

85. (a) Latin, *to say well*: a blessing; the act of blessing

(b) Latin, *vault*: a dark room; a room

(c) Latin, *to please*: affable; self-satisfied

(d) Latin, *seize*: grasp mentally; include, embrace

(e) Latin, *pour together*: to amaze, mix together; mix indiscriminately

86. (a) Latin, *to pile up together*: to explain, interpret; to build

(b) Latin, *burst, break, crack*: a small crack; a deep crack in a glacier

(c) Latin, *to strike*: to ward off, parry; to protect

(d) Latin, *day*; daily record

(e) Latin, *envy, grudge*: selfishly grudging in view of the enjoyment of another; expressing or caused by envy or ill will.

87. (a) Latin, *fit*: not fit; not fit to learn quickly

(b) Latin, *say*: to speak a formal charge of crime against some one; to put into words

(c) Latin, *to call on*: to call on; to address

(d) Latin, *to say evil*: a curse; a curse

(e) Latin, *greatest*: a proverb, a saying or opinion of the greatest importance; greatest quantity

88. (a) Latin, *to advise*: a wise adviser; an advisory supervisor

(b) Latin, *metal*: element, such as iron; the material out of which something is made, natural temperament, courage

(c) Latin, *movable*: easily movable; capable of being moved

(d) Latin, *to obey*: submission; courteous bowing of the knee in token of obedience and loyalty

(e) Latin, *word*: release from custody on word of honor; idle talk or words

89. (a) Latin, *penitence*: deliberate suffering by way of atonement; contrition, sorrow for fault or sin

(b) Latin, *to bewail*: the complaining party in a lawsuit; mournful

(c) Latin, *to prick*: distressing, affecting; stinging to the nerves of taste or smell

(d) Latin, *to be able*: powerful; mighty

(e) Greek, *old*: an (old) man in holy orders; an elder of a church

(f) Latin, *to buy back*: price paid for release; recovery of what is pledged

(g) Latin, *to know again*: reconnoitering in order to know a countryside for military purposes; a legal term containing the idea of appearing before a court again for recognition unless a specified act is performed

(h) Latin, *to reject*: to suspend sentence; to rebuke

(i) Latin, *sacred*: a man in charge of a room set apart for sacred vessels; a church janitor

(j) Latin, *to sit to*: to charge with a tax; a sitting or session of a court

90. (a) Latin, *snare*: a long line for catching cattle; a delicate network (made up of snares of thread)

(b) Latin, *worthy*: fastidious; grave demeanor, as if one were worthy

(c) Latin, *stranger*: one treated with the courtesy normally accorded a stranger; unfriendly, because a stranger

(d) Icelandic, *skirt*: an upper garment; a lower garment

(e) Latin, *to bind*: a legal claim on property; a fibrous substance binding the ends of the bones together

(f) Latin, *reason, reckoning*: exercise of the rational faculties; a fixed allowance, reasoned out or reckoned

(g) Latin, *of the same clan*: one not a Jew; well-bred, i. e. , with the manners of one's own clan

(h) *Heart*: hearty, heartfelt

(i) Latin, *hut*: a public house; a tent used as a sanctuary

(j) Latin, *crab*: a tumor, crab-like in its grip; an ulcerous sore, a disease of trees

91. (a) Both mean "blessing", but *benison* is poetic and quaint and *benediction* is used especially of the blessing which ends a religious service.

(b) A valet is a gentleman's servant; whereas a varlet is a low menial.

(c) Wrack is wreckage, or seaweed cast ashore; a wreck is a ruin or a shipwreck.

92. (a) Yes, but *crevasse* is applicable only to crevices found in ice.

(b) One who is confounded.

(c) Both a monitor and a mentor act in an advisory capacity, but in addition a mentor superintends; a mentor is usually a wise and faithful friend, whereas a monitor may be merely an impersonal official.

(d) Penance.

(e) Possibly. A pungent odor is one which stings the nerves of the nose; a poignant odor is one which touches the emotions. The same odor could be both pungent and poignant, although ordinarily we think of a poignant odor as being delicate and fragrant.

(f) A sacristan holds a more dignified position than a sexton, for the latter is only a church janitor, while the former has charge of the room which contains the sacred vestments and vessels.

(g) Recognizance.

93. (a) An amiable man is loveable, friendly; an amicable man promotes good will and is peaceable.

(b) One who is complaisant is affable, polite, and desirous of pleasing others; one who is complacent is self-satisfied.

(c) An envious man envies some one; invidious actions are provoked by ill-will or arouse ill-will in others.

(d) A mobile machine is capable of being moved easily; a movable machine is also capable of being moved, but there is no suggestion of ease.

(e) A provident person exercises foresight, especially economically; a prudent person is generally cautious and discreet.

94. (a) An asterisk (*) resembles a star; the "science" of stars; a disaster suggests that the stars are ill disposed toward a certain person or event.

(b) having double life (on land and water); a writing about some one's life; the study of life

(c) marriage with two persons at the same time; marriage to one only; marriage with many at the same time.

(d) origin (of a race); record of descent (of a race); something "born inside" — a plant that grows by the accretion of new tissue in the midst of tissue already formed, the plant thus being born into its race.

(e) rule of one who himself holds all the power; rule by the strength of the best men; one who believes in rule by the strength of the people; one who rules by the power of wealth

95. (a) Something written by oneself; stone-written (a process of printing which originally always used a porous stone in the process); written far off; written anew, a rearrangement of the letters of a word so as to create another word; a pithy saying written upon some subject; a plan written across

(b) the outer layer of skin; having a thick skin. Yes, a pachyderm such as an elephant has an outer layer of skin, an epidermis. A human being who is worthy of being called a pachyderm is probably too thick-skinned to appreciate the insult.

(c) a raising of some one to godly rank or honor; denial of God; worship of all the gods, or a belief that God exists in all things; government by God, or His representatives; the study of God

(d) a vault hidden under a church or elsewhere; certain uncanonical books of the Old Testament, i. e., hidden things; a cipher whose meaning is hidden; a series of plants whose means of fructification is "hidden"

(e) something similar to something else (*logos* here means "proportion"; a list which tells, or says, fully; ten sayings, i. e. the Ten Commandments; conversation, speech between two or more persons; the process of reasoning, demonstrated or suggested by the ability to speak; a soliloquy, words spoken when one is alone; words spoken before something else by way of introduction; the study of the stars; the study of God or religion; the science of animals.

96. (a) Greek, *alone, single*: one who rules alone; an indestructible unit; a musical instrument with a single string; an aeroplane with one set of wings; two or more letters woven into one single design

(b) Greek, *measure*: a weight-measure, an instrument designed to measure atmospheric pressure; an instrument which measures amperage; an earth-measurer, one skilled in geometry

(c) Greek, *name*: bearing no name; the naming of a thing after one of its attributes; the making of a name in imitation of a sound; a name derived from one's father or ancestor; a fictitious name; a name (or adjective) like another name or some one

(d) Greek, *feeling*: a feeling against; a feeling in harmony with; the state of being unfeeling or insensitive

(e) Greek, *rock*: to turn into rock; oil from rock

(f) Greek, *time*: an error concerning the time of an event; the history of events in the order of their time; the science of time; a clock, a time-measurer; having equal intervals of time; occurring at the same time

(g) Greek, *wisdom*: a wise-foolish person (!); a lover of wisdom; wise in the ways of the world

(h) Greek, *love*: love of mankind; the city of brotherly love; a lover of England and things English; a love of wisdom

(i) Greek, *fear*: fear of water, one symptom of rabies; hatred or dread of England; fear of enclosed places

97 — 101 No key is furnished to these exercises because a key would destroy their value.

102. (a) to lose one's head
   (b) to have a good head on one's shoulders
   (c) to have a big, or swelled, head
   (d) to take into one's head
   (e) to talk one's head off
   (f) to make head against
   (g) to go, or get in, over one's head

103. (a) to have the face to
   (b) to set one's face against
   (c) to make a face, or faces
   (d) to face someone or something out; to face the music
   (e) to show one's face
   (f) to face someone with
   (g) to have two faces

104. (a) to be all eyes, to have an eye for, in the public eye, to shut one's eyes to, to see with half an eye, up to the eyes, more than meets the eye, a sight for sore eyes
   (b) before one's nose, to lead by the nose, to poke one's nose

into, to look down one's nose, to follow one's nose, to see no further than one's nose

(c) up to one's ears, to set by the ears, to have some one's ear, to be all ears, to play by ear, to prick up one's ears, to go in one ear and out the other

(d) to take the words out of one's mouth, to live from hand to mouth, to give mouth to, by word of mouth, down in the mouth, to make a wry mouth, to laugh on the wrong side of one's mouth

(e) To have a sweet tooth, to cut one's eye-teeth, to get one's teeth into something, to be armed to the teeth, to set one's teeth on edge

105. (a) to have on the tip of one's tongue, to keep a civil tongue in one's mouth, to have a smooth tongue, to hold one's tongue, to have a sharp tongue

(b) to run in the blood, hot-blooded, to breed ill blood, to thirst for blood, to stir the blood, to act in cold blood

(c) to win some one's heart, to have a hard heart, to warm the cockles of the heart, to put one's heart into, to set one's heart on, to lose heart

(d) to get out of hand, to keep one's hand in, to force the hand, to come to hand, in a turn of the hand, to have the upper hand, to hold one's hand, to lend a hand

(e) to cut the ground from under some one's feet, to have one foot in the grave, to put one's foot down, to put one's best foot forward, to set on foot, to be carried off one's feet, to put one's foot into it

106. (a) to give up one's guide

(b) to provide a safeguard

(c) to refuse to surrender

(d) to reveal one's true character or purpose

(e) to resist successfully the force of something

(f) completely lost, bewildered

(g) devoid of resources

(h) to pursue a somewhat more conservative or prudent course

107. (a) to reject another's control
   (b) to aid
   (c) with almost exhausted resources
   (d) completely under control
   (e) to find fault with a gift or something free
   (f) to suffer an accident or setback
   (g) to let another have control

108. (a) to subject to training or experience
   (b) everything is of use
   (c) to assume too many tasks at once
   (d) at full capacity
   (e) to have private ends which one wishes to accomplish
   (f) not to be too critical or too precise
   (g) a process or procedure that begins with small devices and methods but that has the expectation of later employing larger, more forceful, or more spectacular devices
   (h) a child who takes after his father or mother; any one or anything which has marked resemblances to its figurative parent
   (i) to restrict oneself to the business, trade, or activity which he knows best; to avoid meddling outside the field in which one is skilled

109. (a) habitually conforming one's habits and manners to the companion of the moment
   (b) an error
   (c) judged
   (d) delusions, shams
   (e) a task undertaken out of enthusiasm and without expectation of pecuniary reward
   (f) a favorite
   (g) the luxuries of prosperity (with an opprobrious connotation)
   (h) to agree thoroughly with
   (i) to be scrupulous in trifles, to be over-scrupulous
   (j) to have an unsound foundation

110. (a) to deal fairly, impartially; to recognize the merits of some one who has outstanding faults

(b) artlessly to display one's feelings

(c) to perform a useful, usually humble, function

(d) a predetermined outcome

(e) greediness, especially for money

(f) the pursuit of pleasure, especially sinful

(g) by nature or by training well fitted

(h) moral lessons from nature

(i) a good thing which the ignorant are unable to appreciate

111. (a) to pursue; to remove or steal; to advance toward; to go away; to steal; to discern, to draw up, or to write out; to re-build, or to convey property to; to become reconciled; to approach, or to curry favor with

(b) to bestow; to retreat; to issue; to surrender; to surrender to; to be exhausted, or to publish; to transfer, or to cease; to surrender; having a habit of

(c) to loiter in the vicinity of; to be timid or reluctant; to persist; to threaten or worry one; to display; to pay close attention to

(d) to turn; to abandon or renounce; to put in its place; to return; to lay up; to quell; to send, or to start out; to advance; to install, or to interpose; to postpone; to don; to inconvenience, to extinguish, to start from shore, or to disconcert; to build, to raise, or to lodge a guest; to burden *unfairly*; to propose

(e) to turn around, to undertake; to pursue; to oppose; to advance; to err; to return; to precede; to pass; to descend; to issue; to leave; to continue; to be extinguished, to mix in society, or to issue from a building; to review, to rehearse, or to change sides; to examine, to penetrate, to experience, or to perform from beginning to end; to succumb; to ascend; to accompany

(f) to resemble or to pursue; to talk to in private; to remove, to humble pride, or to write from dictation; to mistake; to mimic or to leave; to undertake, or to assume violent grief; to conceive a liking for; to deceive; to lift, to absorb, to interrupt, to enter upon, or to make a protege of some one.

114. Not moral; not colored; hard ("not soft"); susceptible of developing without impregnation ("not married"); doubtful ("not knowing"); eternal ("not withering"); a general pardon from a government ("not remember"); bloodlessness ("not blood"); making insensible of pain ("not perceive"); absence of government ("not a head"); a story, originally for private circulation ("not published"); a pain-reliever ("not pain"); irregular, exceptional ("not the same"); bearing no name ("not name"); lack of feeling ("not suffer or feel"); free from disease germs, non-putrefying ("not rot"); without sex ("not sexual"); suffocation ("not pulse"); having a defect of the eye which prevents rays from converging to a point on the retina ("not mark").

115. An ambassador is one sent around; to amputate is to lop off round about; *ambidexterous* means "right-handed on both sides"; an amphitheatre gives one a view from both sides; *ambiguous*, "having a double meaning," comes from words meaning "driving around"; *ambient* means "moving around"; *amphibious*, "living both on land and in water", literally means "life on both sides"; and an amphora, a two-handled jar, is "carried around".

116. *Antediluvian* means "before the flood"; *antedate* means "to occur before something else"; *antepenultimate* means "before the last but one of a series"; and an ancestor is someone who has gone before someone else in the process of life.

117. The antarctic is opposite to the arctic. An anticlimax is the opposite of a climax. An antidote is a remedy given against the effects of poison or disease. An antimacassar is a covering for the backs of chairs as a protection against soiling by oil from the hair. An antinomian is one whose faith makes him opposed to obedience to the moral law. Antipathy is feeling against some one or something. An antiphon is a musical response (by voice) against the musical utterance of another voice. The antipodes are opposite to one's foot, that is, on the other side of the world. An antiseptic is valuable against "rotting." An antithesis, the direct contrary, is literally "against a place" or "opposite to a place". An antitoxin is good against poison. And an antitype, "against a type", is that which is suggested or foretold by a type.

118. An automobile is self-moving, and so is an automaton; an autopsy, a post-mortem examination of a body, implies that some one sees with his own eyes; an autobiography is self-written; an autocrat rules by himself alone; an autograph is self-written; and autonomy is self-government.

119. Having two wheels; a muscle which divides into two heads or sections; a tooth with two fangs or points; every two years; two-leaved; two-pronged; marriage with two mates; two-sided; two-tongued (speaking two languages); the use of two metals as basic money; two-eyed, like opera-glasses; a creature with two feet; a ship having two banks of oars; to cut into two parts; having two folding "doors", like an oyster.

120. A benediction, or blessing, implies speaking well. Benefaction suggests doing well. A benefice is a church living granted through the favor of some one; a person holding a benefice has been "well done by"! A beneficiary is the receiver of a gift; he too is well done by. Benevolent means well-wishing, kind.

121. (a) *Circum-* means "around". Circumambient, means "going around", i. e., "surrounding". *Circumflex* means "bent around"; the following is a circumflex accent, habitually placed above certain vowels in French: (ˆ). *Circumfluent* means "flowing around." *Circumjacent* means "lying around". To circumnavigate is to sail around. *Circumspect*, "look around", means "cautious". A circumvallation is a fortification around something. *To circumvent* means literally "to come around" in the sense of "to outwit".

(b) The idea common to all these words is "together." *Coagulate*, meaning "congeal", has a literal meaning of "drive together". *Corrode* is literally "gnaw together". *Coaxial* means "possessing a common axis together". *Cognate*, related, means literally "born together". A collocutor is a person who talks together with another, and a colloquy is the conversation in which collocutors indulge. A concatenation of events is a series of events linked or chained together. *Concomitant*, meaning "occurring together", has a basic meaning of "together with a comrade". *Confluent* means "flowing together". A congener is a member of the same race (together with others). A conjunction is a word that joins one word or group of words together with another. And consanguinity is kinship together with another.

(c) *Contrapuntal* is a musical term, the adjective of *counterpoint*, which implies the blending of two melodies note against note, or point by point. *To contradict* is to speak against, and *to contravene* is "to come against", that is to defeat, transgress, or oppose.

(d) *De-* means in these words "away from" or "out". To decalcify is to reverse the process ("away from") of turning something into stone by a deposit of lime salts. To desecrate is the opposite ("away from") of to make sacred. To desiccate is to dry out. And *devious* means literally "away from the path".

122. (a) A demigod is a half-god, a demilune is a half-moon (the word is applied to a fortification shaped somewhat like a half moon), and the demimonde is the half-world or the world of women of equivocal reputation.

(b) A dilemna is a difficult situation consisting of a double choice; a disyllable is a two-syllable word; a digraph is a compound of two letters to express one sound; a diploma is a paper folded double; and a diphthong is two vowels which sound together.

(c) A duologue is a conversation between two people; a duumvir is one of two men who rule together; and duplicity is doubleness of speech or intention.

123. (a) *Eugenic* means well-born or having to do with good birth. A euphemism is a mild term ("well-spoken") substituted for a harsher term, as "to pass away" for "to die". Euphony is harmony ("sound well"). Eulogy is praise ("discourse well"). Euphuism is affectation of elegance in one's writing ("well formed," "well shaped"). *Eupeptic* is an adjective which means "pertaining to good digestion". And the Eucalyptus gets its name from the fact that the stamens are well covered by little hoods.

(b) A letter with the same sound as another; of the same kind; a word of the same sound but with a different meaning; having the same construction or importance.

(c) The idea of "between" is common to both words, for intercolumniation is the space between columns, and an interlocutor is a speaker in a conversation between two persons.

(d) *Intramural* means literally "within the walls"; intramural sports in a school, for instance, are sports played by teams made up of pupils within the school.

(e) To juxtapose is to place next to.

124. *Maladroit* means "clumsy", "bad with the right hand"; a malady is a disease, something "badly had"; something which is malapropos is badly to the purpose; malfeasance is ill-doing; malaria is literally bad air; and a malison, a curse, is bad speaking.

125. (a) *Mis-* means "wrong". A misadventure is a "wrong" or unlucky happening. A misnomer is a name wrongly applied. A miscreant is one who, because he has wrong beliefs, acts wrongly and is consequently a vile wretch. Misprision is high misdemeanor, or wrong acting. *Mis-* in misanthrope is not the prefix meaning "wrong" but comes from a word meaning "hate"; a misanthrope is one who hates mankind. *Misalliance, misappropriate,* and *misfeasance* all contain the idea of "wrong"; a misalliance is a wrong or undesirable marriage, to misappropriate is to take wrongly, and misfeasance is the doing of a lawful act in a wrong or unlawful manner.

(b) *Mono-,* meaning single, one, or alone, enters into the meaning of all these words: a monochrome is a painting in a single color; a monody is a song sung alone; monogamy is marriage with one mate; a monolith is a single stone; a monologue is a speech made alone; monometallism is the use of a single metal, such as gold, as a standard for money; a monopoly is exclusive possession of or rights in anything; monotheism is the worship of one god; and a monotone is a single tone.

(c) *Multifarious* means "manifold"; *multipartite* means "having many parts"; and *multiplicity* means "the condition of being many-fold".

(d) That which is nondescript is *not* capable of description; a nonentity is a person or thing of *no* value.

(e) A palimpsest is a parchment which has been written upon again after complete or partial erasure of previous writing. A palindrome is a word so constituted that it reads the same when it is read forward and again when it is read backward. A palinode is a metrical recantation, retraction, or "taking back again". And palingenesis is rebirth (or "birth again") into a higher second life.

126. (a) By chance; to walk through or about; to pass through a filter; to travel through one land after another; continuing through the years; away from faith (*per* here has the sense of "from"); done merely for the sake of getting through; and to pass through.

(b) The point where a planet in going round its course is nearest the sun; the distance around any two-dimensional figure; walking around; the distance around (circumference); an instrument designed for looking around; pillars set around a building.

(c) Marriage with many husbands; many-colored; marriage with many mates; expressed in many languages; the worship of many gods; a word made up of many syllables.

(d) After the flood; after birth; after a meal.

(e) Forewarning; before a meal; act of going before; acquire beforehand; a first name; following before (in the sense of "hind side foremost" and therefore meaning "absurd"); knowing beforehand; a feeling which one has beforehand; taking place before something else.

127. (a) Beyond human, in the sense of "more than human"; beyond the natural; to omit or neglect (literally, "to send beyond")
(b) move backwards; to move backwards; a part of a church behind the choir; a look backward
(c) Half.
(d) Under water; understanding of that which is not expressed ("hearing underneath"); under the skin; lying beneath; under the moon; financial aid granted by a government to a private enterprise (literally, "sitting under" — in order to bolster up); stratum underlying another.
(e) Situated over the eyebrow; more than is necessary ("flowing over"); above the world; above a fixed or usual number; replace ("sit over").

128. Sympathy is literally a "feeling together with". Symmetry is literally "measure together", that is, harmony of proportions.

A symphony is essentially a group of sounds which are in harmony with one another. A symposium is a banquet in which one drinks with others. A syllogism, a logical form of reasoning, means "reckon together". Syntax, the part of grammar dealing with the construction of sentences, means "arrange together with". A synagogue has the essential idea of "lead together with". *Synchronous* ("time with") means "occurring at the same time". To syncopate is to elide or to contract together one letter, or other unit, with another. *Syndicate* means literally "law together". A synod ("way together") is an ecclesiastical council. A synonym is literally a "name together with" another idea or object. A synopsis is a summary of several things considered together with each other.

129. (a) Telegony is the influence (from afar) of a previous father upon a subsequent father's children by the same mother. Telepathy is the communication of ideas from one mind to another without direct contact (from afar). To telegraph is to write from far off. A telephone brings sound from afar. A telescope is an instrument which enables one to see from afar; a microscope, on the other hand, enables one to see small objects.

(b) A trajectory is the path "thrown across" from a gun to a target by a moving projectile. Across the Atlantic. A transept is that portion of a cruciform church which cuts across the main body of the church between the nave and the choir. To transfuse is to pour a fluid from one vessel across into another. To transfigure is to change the outer appearance across into another appearance. *Transitory* means "existing for a short time", just long enough "to go across". To transliterate is to transpose letter by letter across into another language. *Translucent* means "shining through or across". *Transmigration* is a word applied to the passage of a soul from one body across into another. And to transubstantiate is to change a substance across into another.

(c) The idea of "three" is common to these words: a muscle

with three heads or sections; the science of measuring triangles; a three-angled figure; and three-colored.

(d) The meaning common to these words is "one": having one voice or meaning; relating to one side only; having only one chamber; having one horn; having one form only; a mollusk with one valve; turned into one, that is, belonging to the whole world or to all human beings.

130. (a) The idea of "away" is clearly present in *ablution, abnegate, abrogate,* and *abscond*: washing away, deny away, abolish away, and hide oneself away. It is less evident in the other words: *aboriginal* means "native to the soil" and *abstemious* means "self-denying".

(b) *A-* in conjunction with the consonant immediately following it in each of these words had originally the meaning of "to". The meaning is still present in some of the words: an acclivity is a slope upward (to or toward something); an accolade is an embrace (to or about the neck); an accretion is a growth upon or to something; *agnate* means "akin" ("born to"); and alluvium is soil or sand washed down by water ("wash to"). The idea of "to" is less evident in the present meanings of *adumbrate, adventitious* (Latin, "come to"), *afflatus* ("blow to"), *agglomerate, agglutinate,* and *amerce*.

(c) *Ana-* means "anew", "back", "according to", or "up". An anagram is something written anew, that is a word or phrase made up of letters of another word or phrase recombined. An anabaptist is one baptized over again. An anachronism is a chronological error ("time back"). An analogue is anything similar to another ("according to proportion" literally). Analysis is the process of breaking something up into its parts ("loose back again"). An anapest is a metrical foot consisting of two unaccented syllables and one accented syllable, in that order; the word has the idea in it of "striking back". An anathema is a curse, and an aneurism is a tumor.

The force of the prefix has been almost completely forgotten in all except *anagram, anabaptist,* and perhaps *anachronism.*

131. (a) An archbishop is a chief bishop; an archangel is a chief angel; an architect is a chief builder; and an archetype is a first, primitive type.

(b) *Cata-* means "down", "against", "fully", or "under". A catechism, consisting of question and answer, is literally "an echo against". A catacomb is a hollow underneath the ground. A cataclysm is a flood ("wash down"). A catalogue is a list which "says fully". A catapult hurls missiles against a fortification. A cataract, a waterfall, dashes down. Catarrh is a flowing down from the nose. A catastrophe is a down-turning of events. The prefix in the other words has little present vitality.

(c) *Dia-* means "across", "between", "apart", or "through". *Diagram* retains some idea of writing across; *diaphonous* means "showing light through its substance"; a diatribe is invective which "rubs through" the person or thing criticized. The meaning of the prefix is less apparent in the other words.

(d) *Ephemeral, epicycle, epidemic, epidermis, epigram, epilepsy,* and *epithet* retain some of the force of the prefix, which means "upon" or "on". *Ephemeral,* meaning "transitory", suggests existence on one day only. An epicycle is a circle which rolls on or around another circle. An epidemic is a widespread disease which falls on a group of people. An epidermis is a skin on another skin. An epigram is a pithy saying written on some subject. Epilepsy is a disease with paroxysms which seizes on the victim. And an epithet is a descriptive word applied to (put on) someone or something.

(e) *Ex-* retains the idea of "out", "off", or "from" in excogitate (think out), excoriate (skin off), excrescent (growing out), execrate (curse out), exfoliate (peel or scale off), exonerate (remove the burden of blame from), exorcise (cast out an evil spirit), and exude (ooze out).

(f) *Hetero-* means "other" or "different": inflected irregularly, that is, "in another way"; at variance with the usual opinion (literally "other opinion"); made up of different elements.

(g) *Hyper-* means "over": over-statement; very cold (as it is over the extreme northern part of the world); over-growth; over-critical.

(h) A fire-room situated under another for the purpose of warming it; morbid melancholy (the source of which was believed to be under the breast-bone); under the skin; and a supposition underlying some argument or belief. *Hypo-* "under."

(i) *Im-* in *imbrue* means "in": "drink in"; that is, drench. *Im-* in *impeccable* means "not": not sinful.

(j) Metabolism is the change of dead food over into living matter. Metamorphosis is change from one shape over into another. Metempsychosis is transmigration of a soul from one body over into another. The force of *meta-* is less evident in *metaphor* and *metonymy*.

(k) *Ob-* means "to", "near", "against", or "upon". Its force is still evident in *obdurate* ("hard against"; that is, unyielding), in obloquy ("speaking against", that is, defamation), in *obnoxious* ("hurtful to"), and in *opprobrium* ("disgrace upon"). It is less evident in the present meanings of the other words.

(l) Pantomime "imitates all"; that is, it is a play which represents all without the aid of dialogue. A panacea is a cure-all. Pandemonium is the abode of all the demons. A panoply is the complete armor of a warrior. A panorama is a complete view of all in every direction. A pantograph is an instrument for copying a drawing; that is, it "writes all". The pancreas gland ("all flesh") has lost the sense of "all" in its present meaning.

132. (a) *Para-* means "beside", "side by side", "near to", and "contrary to". A parody is a burlesque imitating ("near to") some serious work. A paraclete, specifically the Holy Ghost, is one called near for aid. A paradigm is a pattern for the inflection of a word which shows side by side all the forms of the word. A paradox (literally "contrary to opinion") is an apparently self-contradictory statement.

(b) *Pro-* means "before", "forward", or "for". A proboscis is the extension forward of a nose, like an elephant's trunk. A proclivity is a sloping forward toward something, a natural tendency toward something. To procrastinate is to put off for tomorrow something which can be done today. A profligate dashes forward to vice and dissipation. A progenitor is a forefather. *Prognostic* means "foretelling something which is to occur in the future." A program is something written before an event. A prolocutor is one who speaks for another or before a group. And *prolix* ("flowing forward") means "indulging in wordy discourse."

(c) A protagonist is the first, or leading, person in a play or contest. *Protoplasm* means literally "first molded form" and still contains some suggestion of that idea. And a prototype is a primitive ("first") form.

(d) *Re-* means "again", "in return", "back again", or "over". To recriminate is to accuse in return. To relegate is to send back, to banish. A reagent is an agent which "acts again" in response to a previous action. *Recalcitrant* (literally "kicking back") means "rebellious". A recension is a doing over again, a revision. A recrudescence is the appearance once more (usually of something undesirable or unpleasant). To redintegrate is to make whole again. *Redundant* means "more than required" (literally "flowing again"). *Refrangible*, meaning "capable of refraction", comes from Latin words meaning "break again". That which is refulgent shines back. To regenerate is to generate or form anew. To regurgitate is to throw or pour back again. To reiterate is to repeat again and again. To rejuvenate is to make young again. A renaissance is a rebirth, a "birth again". A renegade is one who "denies back" or renounces his beliefs. Replete, "full to the utmost", means literally "filled again". To retaliate, meaning literally "such again", is to repay like for like. *Re-* has little force now in the present meaning of *reprobate*.

(e) To secede is to withdraw from ("go aside"), and to segregate is to separate, or "set aside from the flock".

(f) A subterfuge, coming from words which mean "flee under", is a false excuse.